Teaching and Testing
Science Process Skills

Teaching and Testing

Science Process Skills

K.P. Suresh
Celene Joseph

SHIPRA

ISBN: 978-81-7541-631-4

First Published in India in 2012

Teaching and Testing Science Process Skills

SHIPRA PUBLICATIONS
H.O.: LG 18-19, Pankaj Central Market, Patparganj,
I.P. Ext., Delhi-110092, Tel: 91-11-2223 5152, 2223 6152
Br.Off.: 4617/18, Ansari Road, Darya Ganj,
New Delhi-110002, Tel: 6594 6453, 9810522367
E-mail: info@shiprapublications.com
www.shiprapublications.com

Preface

This book provides an introduction to the basic concepts of science processes and the process involved in the teaching of science education. Science processes are intellectual skills used in collecting and analysing the data to solve problems. In all modern educational systems, science education is imparted through actual scientific activities—experimentation and organisation of first hand knowledge obtained through experimentation.

It is heavily criticised that science education provided in the Indian schools is pre-dominantly bookish and theoretical. Science disciplines are intended to develop higher order mental abilities. Even in the best schools, science education is carried out on traditional lines, measuring mostly, the students' ability to recall and comprehend the imparted information.

Today, with the emerging trends in science education, processes are given more emphasis, curricula are framed and text books are rewritten with a view to develop science process skills. There is a shift in emphasis from the teaching of science content to that of helping students develop competence in the science process.

The book mainly focuses on the teaching of science education being prescribed at elementary, secondary, higher secondary and higher education realms. We believe that it can provide mind-altering and practical suggestions for those interested in the field of science education imparted at D.Ed., B.Ed., M.Ed. and MA Education classes and for researchers, teacher educators and curriculum developers in the field of science education.

Science can be viewed as an attitude towards life. The acquisition of scientific attitude is one of the most important aims of science teaching and learning. But the extent to which the teaching of science and the learning of the subject is effective in imparting training of skills and acquisition of science processes is in question.

We hope this piece of work will be of immense use for those interested in the teaching of science and will act as a catalyst and a reference book for their pedagogical considerations and cognitive imaginations.

We humbly solicit criticisms and suggestions for improvement, from the readers and practitioners in the field.

K.P. Suresh
Celene Joseph

Contents

Preface v

I. Nature of Science **1**

- Science as Process or Product 2
- 'Science' as Making Sense of the World 3
- Definition of Science 6
- The Nature of Science 7
- Science: A Body of Knowledge 8
- Science: A Method of Inquiry, A Way of Investigation 11
- Scientific Thinking and Critical Thinking 11
- Relationship between Process and Products of Science 12
- Science: An Attitude towards Life, A Way of Thinking 13
- Scientific Literacy 14
- The Role of Science Teacher in Promoting Scientific Literacy 14
- Conclusion 16

II. Major Curricular Innovations Focused on Science Process **17**

- Physical Science Study Committee (PSSC) 18
- Science: A Process Approach (SAPA) 18
- Conceptually Oriented Programme in Elementary Science (COPES) 21
- Minnesota Mathematics and Science Teaching Project (MINNEMAST) 22
- Tennessee Science Curriculum Framework (TSCF) 24
- Tennessee's Four Components of Science Education 25
- Elementary Science Study (ESS) 27
- Elementary-School Science Project (ESSP) 29

- Science Curriculum Improvement Study (SCIS) 30
- Unified Science and Mathematics for Elementary Schools (USMES) 31
- Scientific Thinking (Scottish Education Department Curriculum) 35
- Nuffield Science Curriculum Project 35
- Warwick Science Process 36
- Assessment of Performance Unit (APU) 36
- Science in Process 37
- Conclusion 37

III. Scientific Method **38**

- Scientific Method and its Meaning 39
- Some Elements of Scientific Method 42
- Mill's Canons of Induction 44
- Analogy 49
- Analysis and Synthesis 50
- Hypothesis 51
- Collection of Facts and Data 54
- Observation 54
- Experiment 55
- Scientific Method and Transfer of Training 58
- Application of Scientific Method to the Teaching of Science 58
- Conclusion 59

IV. Science Process Skills **60**

- Emergence of Science as a Process 60
- Significance of Process Skills in Science Teaching 61
- Definition of Process Outcomes 64
- Process vs Product Approach 66
- Science as Problem Solving 68
- Taxonomical Approaches in Defining Educational Objectives 69
- Bloom's Taxonomy of Educational Objectives 69
- Gagne's Hierarchy of Learning Types 72
- Nedelsky's Competence: Ability Classification in Science Learning 73
- Classification in Terms of Science Process Skills 74
- The AAAS Classification of Science Process Skills 75
- Klopfer's Classification of Outcomes in Science 75
- Process of Science (Nay, Marshal and others) 77
- Andrew's Classification (1980) 80
- UNESCO Approach Relating to Process Outcomes 80
- Shepardson's Identification of Science Processes 83

- Process Models 84
- Carin and Sund's Model (1970) 84
- Wilson's Model (1974) 86
- Piaget's Model of Intellectual Development (1963) 86
- Hierarchical Nature of Science Process Skills 88
- Conclusion 90

V. Studies on Process Skills 91

- Research Studies Focussed Focussing on Science Process Skills 91
- Conclusion 106

VI. Teaching of Science Process Skills 107

- Strategies and Sample Lesson Plans for Developing Science Process Skills 107
- Constructivist Teaching Strategy 108

Lesson Plans

- Lesson Plan Based on Constructivist Approach 108
- Lesson Plan Based on Cognitive Apprenticeship Model 115
- Lesson Plan Based on Cognitive Apprenticeship Model 118
- Lesson Plan Using Concept Attainment Model 127
- Lesson Plan Based on Inquiry Training Model 132
- Lesson Plan Based on 7E Learning Cycle 141
- Lesson Plan Based on Goal Based Scenario Model 149
- Lesson Plan Using Problem Based Learning Strategy 157

VII. Testing of Science Process Skills 161

- Direct and Indirect Assessment 162
- Techniques for Performance Based Assessment 163
- Science Journals 165
- Inquiry Reports 166
- Investigation Reports 167
- Test of Process Outcomes in Physics 168
- Test of Process Outcomes in Physics 177

References 198

Index 211

I

Nature of Science

The progress and prosperity of any nation is determined by its advancements in science and technology, which is an outcome of the science education imparted to its younger generation. The advancements of the developed countries provide ample evidences for this fact. Understanding the prime importance of science education in the advancement of any nation is well conceived by the developed and developing countries. They are now attempting to improve their science education by restructuring it to fit in with the needs, challenges and expectations of its citizens.

National Policy on Education (1992) states, "....Science educators have the role of providing such scientifically literate citizens to the nation. To fulfil its expectations, citizens should be scientifically literate, skilled in the processes of science, acquire scientific information in depth and cultivate an appreciation for science".

There is a shift in emphasis from the teaching of science content to that of helping students develop competence in the science processes. *Science processes* are intellectual skills used in collecting and analysing data to solve problems. In all modern educational systems, science education is given through actual scientific activities—experimentation and organization of first hand knowledge obtained through experimentation.

The conservative content-led approach is proved inadequate to meet the needs since it does not equip the learners to acquire the intended understanding of scientific knowledge and to apply this knowledge effectively in familiar and unfamiliar contexts and in problem solving situations. Majority fails to attain mastery over school science. Only a tiny minority of pupils gain a meaningful understanding of science, which helps them to use their knowledge effectively and creatively. If the teachers are using inquiry approaches in teaching science, it gives teachers, the opportunity to develop student abilities and to enrich student understanding of science. When students focus on the processes of inquiry, they develop the ability to ask questions, define problems, investigate the world around them and use their observations to construct reasonable explanations for the problem.

Science as Process or Product

Beginning from the 1960 numerous curriculum innovations have laid stress on scientific procedures and on the development of scientific attitudes. Some of these innovations emphasize the scientific processes at the expense of products and others advocate the teaching of products through processes. The swing between processes and products had been a controversial issue for a long time. Considering the historical precedents and future applications of this swing, it is high time adopt a proper stand regarding the central concern of science education.

Today, with the emerging trends in science education, processes are given more stress, curricula are framed and text-books are rewritten with a view to develop science process skills. But the extent to which teaching and learning is effective in imparting training in the development of skills and acquisition of knowledge is in question. This effectiveness depends on individual variables belonging to the cognitive and affective domains, social variables and the variables related to the immediate environment of the learner.

In order to promote the development of process skills among children, the Commission on Science Education of the American Association for the Advancement of Science (AAAS) launched a programme entitled "Science: A Process Approach" (SAPA). This programme is now getting momentum in the Indian context too. The National Policy on Education (NPE, 1986) emphasized a child centred science curriculum, stresses the need for an activity based learning of science, especially, in the primary stage. The curriculum is so framed as to develop process skills in children. The textbooks contain learning experiences, which promote scientific inquiry.

The skills of scientific inquiry or investigation have a general and transferable nature; individuals can use them in solving problems concerning other subject areas or problems that arise in real life. But the reality that no process can exist without content should also be taken into account. Hence, the science education oriented to face the demands of tomorrow's unknown dimensions should have a harmonious blend of processes and product, with special emphasis on the processes of science.

The call for placing science processes in the central position of science education began with Dewey's teaching on the utility value of education in 1920s. It geared momentum in 1960s. New science curricula that are being framed all over the world, lay major emphasis on the investigative and exploratory phases of science, which helping the development of inquiry skills. Now, a major concern of all the developed and developing countries is to improve the quality of science education imparted to its students.

'Science' as Making Sense of the World

The recent curricular innovations stress 'science' as making sense of the world. This is consistent with what the scientists see as they actually perform in their scientific investigations. It humanizes 'science' as scientific competencies or skills that all curricula strive to develop in pupils. The skills included in the curricula are important means by which children can make better sense of their world. Children should get help in developing such skills at the time when they are in need of assistance to solve problems.

This change in the concept of science should reflect in the goals of science teaching, in the methods and techniques used for science teaching, in the development of curriculum, n the preparation of instructional materials and in the evaluation procedures. The change in the trend from product to process leads the learners to be well-versed in the methods of scientific investigation, there by generating a scientific attitude.

This shift in emphasis from the product of science to process has some basic roots in the statements of the educational objectives given by Bloom, (1968) and Klopfer, (1971), in the learning hierarchy of Gagne, (1985), and in the stages of cognitive development enunciated by Piaget (1963). In Bloom's classification of educational objectives, the behaviours that come under the sub-domains—comprehension, application, analysis, synthesis and evaluation—are concerned directly or indirectly with science process skills.

In Klopfer's classification of educational outcomes, the four categories, namely, observing and measuring, seeing a problem and seeking ways to solve it, interpreting data and formulating generalisations, building, testing and revising a theoretical model constitute some of the basic and integrated science process skills. Similarly, in Gagne's (1985) hierarchy of learning types, the intellectual skills lead an individual to the proficiency of thinking skills. Piaget gives a picture of the sequential arrangement of these intellectual skills in his cognitive development theory.

The modern science curricula which are framed after the learning theories highlight the discovery, investigatory and inquiry approaches with special emphasis to the science process skills. This shift from content to process is evident in the way science is practised in many advanced systems.

In all modern educational systems, science education is imparted through actual scientific activities—sensing the problem, formulation of hypothesis, testing of hypothesis by designing and conducting experiments, collecting data, and organisation of first hand knowledge obtained through experiments. But in our schools and colleges, science education is provided through the simulated experimental situations, where experiments designed by some others are replicated and the already existing inference are drawn newly. These simulated experimental opportunities are totally inadequate to take the learner into the heart of the experimental situations.

The real experiment implies sensing the problem by the individual, translating it into the operational problem situation, suggesting probable solution to the problem and designing experiments to test the validity of the tentative solutions. Further it involves controlling and manipulating the variables involved in the actual experimental situation, conducting the experiment, collecting data and drawing inference from the experiment. The mental processes involved in the above said sequence of actions are too complex to be acquired as a by-product of conventional methods of teaching and experimentation. It results in the passive acquisition of second hand knowledge that the learner will never be able to use. In order to lead the situation to actual experimental situation, the science course should be planned in such a way that, the pupils should go to the laboratory just as the scientists do and find out facts which are not new to the world, but new to them through appropriate observation and experimentation.

Science education in the Indian schools has deviated much from this direction. It is criticised as it is predominantly bookish and theoretical. Science disciplines intend to develop higher mental abilities in students has given the same status as that of other disciplines. Even in the best schools, science education is carried out on traditional lines. Teachers evaluate students' performance by using conventional instruments, which measure mostly their abilities to recall and comprehend the imparted information.

Many attempts have been made in India, following the shift from product to process that had taken place all over the world. The curriculum has been reframed on the basis of sound psychological and pedagogical principles, placing emphasis on first hand experiences of students and development of process skills. Textbooks were written on these lines. But in the Indian context, these curriculum reformations are seemed to be ineffective in most of the cases as the infrastructural facilities of majority of schools are inadequate. Without a well-equipped laboratory or subject room, the extent of the attainment of inquiry skills will be limited. Moreover, the science teachers themselves should possess the inquisitiveness and skills in science processes in order to foster them among their students.

The acquisition of process skills is characterised by the proficiency in dealing with many of its component skills, comprising of sensing and defining a problem, observing, measuring, classifying, using numbers, using space-time relationships, communicating, predicting, inferring, defining operationally, formulating hypothesis, interpreting data, controlling variables and experimenting.

Discovery, inquiry and investigative approaches in science education are different in their nature and application. The new curriculum developments in science all over the world emphasises the teaching of science as inquiry. Traditionally science has been taught as a body of knowledge to be jam-packed into the memory of the students. The inquiry approach does not promote the amassing of authoritative information. It is more concerned with discovering new information through scientific activities related to discovery.

Inquiry is a terminal thinking process in which the student has to actively engage in, after passing through the necessary prerequisites for conducting it. Broad, generalized knowledge should be envisaged by the learners as knowledge of principles. Therefore, it should be attained in the context of teaching and learning conditions which include discovery from the part of the learner. It cannot be attained in a superficial manner or through drill and practice without the active involvement of the individual. Hence an active involvement of the learner is a prerequisite for the successful practice of inquiry. According to Bruner, inquiry is in its essence a matter of rearranging or transforming evidence in such a way that one is enabled to go beyond the evidence so reassembled to the new.

Definition of Science

The word science originated from the Latin word 'Scientia' which means knowledge. Science is a systematized body of knowledge. Science has been defined in different fashions. Huxley defines science as organized common sense. Henry Poincore defines science as 'a heap of truth.' According to Fitz Patrick, (1959) "Science is a cumulative and endless series of empirical observations, which result in the formation of concepts and theories, with both concepts and theories subject to further empirical observations. Science is both a body of knowledge and a process of acquiring it." Conant defines science as "An interconnected series of concepts and conceptual schemes that have developed as a result of experimentation and observation and are truthful for further experimentation and observation"

Columbia encyclopaedia has given a working definition for science. "Science is an accumulated and systematized learning in general usage restricted to natural phenomena. The progression in science is marked not only by the accumulation of knowledge, but by the emergence of scientific method and of scientific attitude". According to B.F. Skinner, "Science is first of all a set of attitudes. It is a disposition to deal with facts, rather than with what some one has said about them. The true nature of science is revealed as a way it is sought, rather than what is found." Gagne defines science as 'What Scientists do'.

The analysis of definitions of science reflects its multi-facets. These are:

1. Science—a body of knowledge
2. Science—a method of inquiry, a way of investigation
3. Science—an attitude towards life, a way of thinking

The Nature of Science

Communicating the nature of science is now considered as one of the general goals of science education. In its project 2061, the AAAS identifies the nature of science as one of four categories of knowledge, skills, and attitudes essential for all citizens. Three principal aspects of nature of science are emphasized:

The Scientific World View: The world is understandable, scientific ideas can change, scientific knowledge is longstanding, and science cannot provide complete answers to all questions.

Scientific Methods of Inquiry: Science demands evidence, science blends logic and imagination, science explains and predicts, scientists try to identify and avoid bias and science is not authoritarian.

The Nature of Scientific Enterprise: Science is a complex social activity, science is organized in to content disciplines and is conducted in various institutions. Ethical principles govern the conduct of science, and scientists participate in public affairs both as specialists and as citizens (AAAS, 1990).

So the nature of science can be listed as follows:

1. Science is constantly, systematically and usually revisionary
2. The tenets of science are constantly changing and profounder of science are under challenge also.
   e.g. 1. Big Bang theory vs. Continuous explosion theory.
   e.g. 2. Law of conservation of mass was modified after Einstein's theory of relativity as law of conservation of Mass Energy.
3. Findings of science have a bearing on the customs and civil laws of man.
4. Science searches for data and other meanings.

Science: A Body of Knowledge

Science can be seen as a body of knowledge/content obtained by scientists as a product of their search for truth/investigations. This body of knowledge includes terms, facts, concepts, laws, theories, principles, formulae and symbols.

Terms: Terms in science are the words or phrases used as the name of concepts, processes, equipments, phenomena etc.

e.g. catalyst, simple combination, double decomposition, microscope, refraction etc.

Facts: According to Oxford advanced learner's dictionary "Fact is something known to be true or accepted as true." James B. Conant gives two criteria for facts. They are:

1. A fact must be directly observable
2. A fact must be directly demonstrable

e.g. 1. The colour of $CuSO_4$ is sky-blue.

e.g. 2. The lines in sun's spectrum correspond to lines in the spectrum of helium.

The statement "Sun contains Helium is a conclusion drawn from comparison of solar spectrum and the spectrum of Helium, not a fact.

Concept: Concept is an abstract or general idea inferred or derived from specific instances

A concept is assumed to be a generalized idea regarding a set of specific objects, symbols or events which share common characteristics (critical attributes) and can be referred by a particular name or symbol. It is a classification of ideas, objects or events into a 'set' by mentally abstracting the common characteristics (attributes which defines that set), e.g. animal, atom, mineral etc.

According to Bruner there are five elements for a concept. They are:

- Examples
- Attributes (characteristics of the concept)
- Attribute range: The range of variation of characteristics
- Name: The term which use to denote the concept

- Definition: Verbal explanation of the concept (which includes the relationship between essential attributes)

Law/Rule: According to Gagne "relationship between two or more concepts is a law/rule. A scientific *law* is a hypothesis that is assumed to be universally true. A law has good predictive power, allowing a scientist (or engineer) to model a physical system and predict what will happen under various conditions.

For Example: 1. Ohm's law 2. Boyle's law

Principle: A higher order law or rule is a principle. They are more complex ideas than a law and is based on several concepts. It is a broad generalization which means same for all the people, irrespective of their age and experience and holds good in different situations.

For Example: Le Chatlier's principle, Archimedes principle.

Framework, Model, Theoretical Account: A hypothetical description of a complex entity or process.

For Example: "The computer programme was based on a model of the circulatory and respiratory systems".

Theory: An idea or set of ideas that is intended to explain something. Theory is a well-substantiated explanation of some aspect of the natural world; an organized system of accepted knowledge that applies in a variety of circumstances to explain a specific set. It is a set of statements, including laws and hypotheses that explain a group of observations or phenomena in terms of those laws and hypotheses. A theory thus accounts for a wider variety of events than a law does. Broad acceptance of a theory comes when it has been tested repeatedly on new data and has been used to make accurate predictions. Although a theory generally contains hypotheses that are still open to revision, sometimes it is hard to know where the hypothesis ends and the law or theory begins. Albert Einstein's theory of relativity, for example, consists of statements that were originally considered to be hypotheses (and daring at that time). But all the hypotheses of relativity have now achieved the authority of scientific laws, and Einstein's theory has supplanted Newton's laws of motion. In some cases, such as the germ theory of infectious disease, a theory becomes so completely accepted, it stops being referred to as a theory.

Theorem: A general conclusion required to be proved on the basis of given assumptions.

Hypothesis: It is statement that explains or makes generalizations about a set of facts or principles, usually forming a basis for possible experiments to confirm its viability. It is a tentative insight into the natural world; a concept that is not yet verified, but if it is true, would explain certain facts or phenomena; "a scientific hypothesis that survives experimental testing becomes a scientific theory". Thus a hypothesis is:

- a tentative explanation for an observation, phenomenon, or scientific problem that can be tested by further investigation.
- something taken to be true for the purpose of argument or investigation; an assumption.
- the antecedent of a conditional statement.
- a principle or proposition that is assumed for the sake of argument or that is taken for granted to proceed to the proof of the point in question.
- a system or theory created to account for something that is not understood.

A hypothesis is a proposition that attempts to explain a set of facts in a unified way. It generally forms the basis of experiments designed to establish its plausibility. Simplicity, elegance, and consistency with previously established hypotheses or laws are also major factors in determining the acceptance of a hypothesis. Though a hypothesis can never be proven true (in fact, hypotheses generally leave some facts unexplained), it can sometimes be verified beyond reasonable doubt in the context of a particular theoretical approach. New hypotheses inconsistent with well-established laws are generally rejected, barring major changes to the approach. An example is the law of conservation of energy, which was firmly established but had to be qualified with the revolutionary advent of quantum mechanics and the uncertainty principle.

Science: A Method of Inquiry, A Way of Investigation

Science is not merely a collection of facts, concepts, and useful ideas about nature, or even the systematic investigation of nature. Science is a method of exploring nature that discovers reliable knowledge about it. Science is a method of discovering reliable knowledge about nature. There are other methods of discovering and learning knowledge about nature, but science is the only method that results in the acquisition of reliable knowledge.

Process aspects reflect the ways in which scientists work. These are the methods or approaches through which scientists find out new knowledge and students acquire them. The processes of science have been defined as, "the characteristics of the activities and scientist's methods of analysis". In other words, these are the methods which scientists practice while searching new knowledge, doing laboratory work or conducting some experiments. These involve from simple observation to the development of a theoretical model. e.g. Observation is one of such process and experimenting is another process. All these processes involve many sub processes which can be systematically arranged in an order, from simple to complex. The processes are essential part of students' learning experiences so that they can learn and practice the methodology of science.

Scientific Thinking and Critical Thinking

When we use the scientific method to study or explore nature we practice scientific thinking. As scientists actively studying nature and investigating the universe by using the scientific method, they practice scientific thinking. When we use the methods and principles of scientific thinking in different activities in everyday life, we practice critical thinking. Critical thinking is the thinking strategy that successfully leads to the most authentic solutions to problems. It gives you reliable knowledge about all aspects of life and society, and is not restricted to the formal study of science.

Scientific thinking is the same in theory and practice, but the term would be used to illustrate the method that gives trustworthy knowledge about the natural world. Undoubtedly, scientific and critical thinking are the same way of thinking, but scientific thinking is always practiced by scientists. On the other hand, critical thinking is used by humans in all walks of life. The scientific method has proven to be the most reliable and successful method of thinking.

Relationship between Process and Products of Science

While we view science as a method inquiry or a way of investigation, we focus on its dynamic nature. It does not overlook the view point that science is a body of knowledge but it emphasizes that body of knowledge is a part of science. Scientific method is the method followed by the scientists in their investigation or search for truth. This aspect is also known as process aspect of science. The process aspect concerns with what scientists do and product aspect concerns with what scientists know. These aspects are interdependent. They are often referred as subject and method, content and activities, knowledge and behaviour etc.

Product

- Terms
- Facts
- Concepts
- Law/Rule
- Principle
- Framework, model, theoretical
- Account
- Theory
- Theorem
- Hypothesis
- Formulae

Process

- Observing
- Using
  Space/Time Relationship
- Classifying
- Using numbers
- Measuring
- Communicating
- Predicting
- Inferring
- Integrated Processes
- Controlling Variables
- Interpreting Data
- Formulating Hypotheses
- Defining Operationally
- Experimenting

Fig. 1.1: Processes and Products of Science

Actually the products of science are the result of processing science or doing science. When a researcher or learner observes a phenomena, he gathers information. When he measures physical quantified qualities we will get data. When he draws inference from the observed data, the result is inference. When he postulates the most suitable solution or explanation to a scientific phenomenon, the result is hypothesis. So the processes and products are closely inter-dependent and cannot be overlooked in science instruction. If both these aspects are not finding due emphasis in science instruction, the result will be a handicapped learning outcome.

Science: An Attitude towards Life, A Way of Thinking

Science can be viewed as an attitude towards life. The acquisition of scientific attitude is one of the most important aims of science teaching and learning. An attitude is a mind set or mental disposition to act favourably or against some objects, events, ideas or enterprises. It is difficult to define scientific attitude. But it is manifested by the characteristics of the person who holds it. The characteristics of a person who possesses scientific attitude are as follows:

- Open mindedness
- Curiosity
- Belief in cause-effect relationship
- Freedom from superstitions
- Intellectual honesty
- Objectivity
- Willingness to change belief if evidence is there
- Respect others' opinion if convincing
- Make judgments based on scientific facts
- Critical mindedness
- Methodical way of solving problems
- Up-to-datedness
- Ability to discern between facts and fission

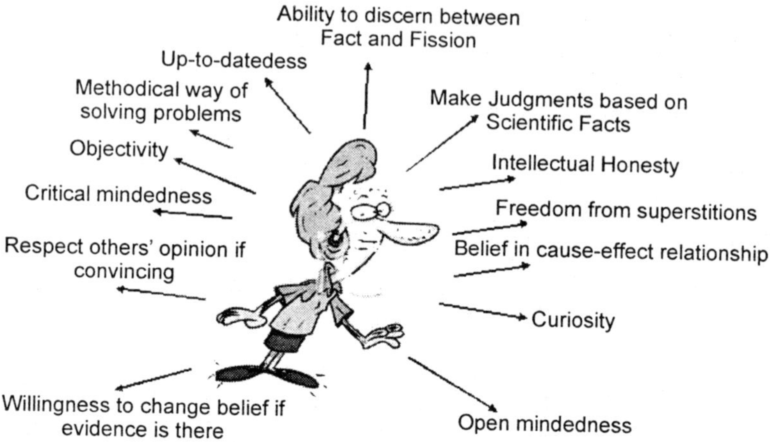

Fig.1.2: A Man of Scientific Attitude

Scientific Literacy

Scientific literacy means a clear understanding of the nature of science and the inter-relationship between science, technology and society (Fig. 1.3). These include:

- a good scientific knowledge base—the knowledge of the content of science with the ability
- a sound understanding of the nature of science
- a positive attitude to science and technology
- the ability to make value judgments and decisions on science based societal issues
- skill in the processes of science
- the ability to use scientific method in solving problems
- a better understanding of the world around as a result of science instruction

The Role of Science Teacher in Promoting Scientific Literacy

The science teacher is a single most important means to promote scientific literacy. In order to achieve this, he/she should have the following characteristics:

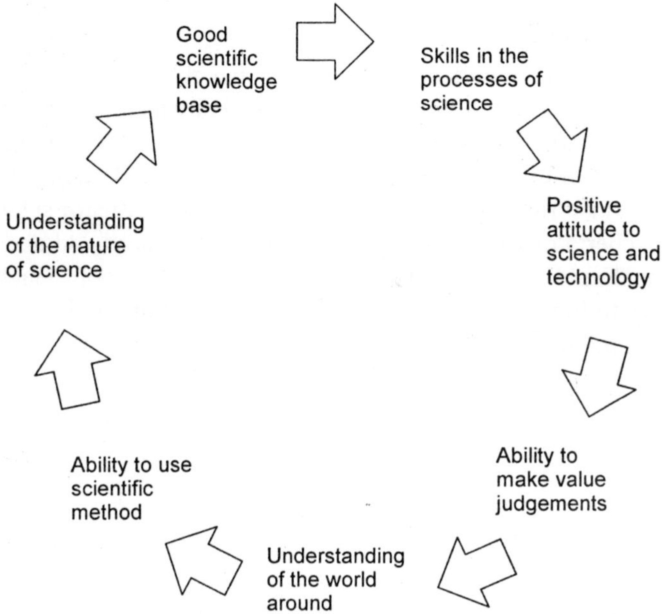

Fig. 1.3: Scientific Literacy

- Should have mastery over the subject matter
- Should keep abreast with the latest technological developments
- Should have a good understanding of the nature of science
- Should be enthusiastic in facilitating learning experiences so as to equip the students with inquiry skills
- Should provide learning experiences which build positive attitude towards life
- Should develop value judgement among students regarding science based issues in daily life
- Should develop among students the ability to study the interaction of science, technology and society
- Should emphasise the technological applications of science that benefit society
- Should point out the moral and ethical implications of science and society
- Should stress the need for having personal values related to science and societal issues

Conclusion

Science teacher should deal lessons so that the nature of science pervades instruction. Science as a body of knowledge, a method of inquiry, an attitude towards life and a way of thinking should be emphasized in the teaching and learning of science. Teacher should sense the historical, developmental and cultural aspects of science.

Teacher's instructions, students' activities, and guided and free inquiry should be included in the purview of classroom teaching. These activities serve to develop scientific attitude and scientific literacy among students.

II

Major Curricular Innovations Focused on Science Process

Since 1960, the teaching of science became a major concern that and it has received global attention. This period was one that of intense and vigorous development of science curriculum marked by the publication of many major projects. The major curricular innovations launched as a revolt against the traditional product-led approach stressed the development of processes in science teaching. Physical Science Study Committee (PSSC), Science: A Process Approach (SAPA), Harvard Physics Project (HPP), Elementary Science Study (ESS), Science Curriculum Improvement Study (SCIS), Elementary School Science Project (ESSP), School Science Curriculum Project (SSCP), Minnesota Mathematics and Science Teaching Project (MINNEMAST), Conceptually Oriented Programme in Elementary Science (COPES), Chemical Education Material Study (CHEMSTUDY), Chemical Bond Approach (CBA), Science in Process, Warwick Process Science, various Nuffield courses in the UK and ASEP in Australia are some of them.

Programmes such as SCIS, SAPA, ESS and COPES were emerged in the United States and these marked a historical twist in science curriculum design for elementary schools. The development of scientific literacy beginning with the youngest pupils was the focus of national attention of United States while designing these curricula. The nation backed up its interest with national funding, the very best scientific minds of top universities began to ask how children could be prepared for a world that needs, not only scientists but citizens capable of dealing with the political, social and economic impact of ongoing scientific progress. Public funds were made available for nationwide curriculum development, testing, revision, retesting and re-revision with concomitant ongoing teacher training and support of the teacher in the classroom. The teachers were given science lessons that were good science involving hands-on science learning, based on solid psychological principles, and thoroughly tested in diverse classrooms. The major portion of this unique educational experiment took place from about 1965 to 1975.

A recurring and significant feature of most of these curriculum proposals was a major shift in emphasis away from the teaching of science as a body of established knowledge, towards science as a human activity with increasing emphasis on the process and procedure of science. The curriculum projects are framed in such a way that, children should enjoy science through direct engagement in scientific activities and gain an awareness of what scientists do and should be engaged to pursue the study of science at an advanced level. A critical evaluation of these reveals that, the intensity of the role of processes are different, but they have some uniqueness. Some of the major curricular studies are detailed by the Fig. 2.1.

Physical Science Study Committee (PSSC)

Physical Science Study committee (PSSC) was formed in 1956 which devised new Physics texts, laboratory manuals, films and supplementary reading materials. In its preamble, it is was claimed that science teaching is made process oriented and due stress is laid on discovery learning and conceptual schemes of science.

The emphasis given in this programme were

- on helping children learn science information, skills, attitudes.
- characteristics of science processes and products.
- teaching science through discovery approach.

Science: A Process Approach (SAPA)

Science: A Process Approach (SAPA) is was an experimental programme in elementary school science, Kindergarten through

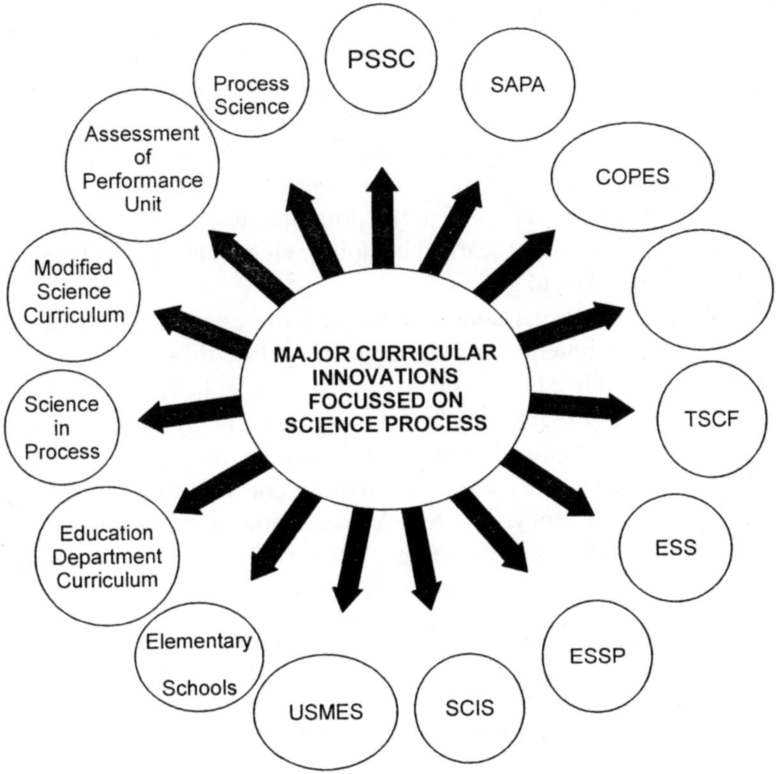

Fig. 2.1: Major Curricular Innovations Focused on Science Process

Grade 6, sponsored by the American Association for the Advancement of Science (AAAS). The AAAS Commission on Science Education began its work in 1962 with funding from the National Science Foundation. The programme was developed by teams consisting of scientists and educators. The Commission's experiment in science education emphasized carefully stated and tested behavioural objectives for each lesson and identifies a hierarchy of tasks for achievement of competence in each of the eight process skills. This programme was highly organized and tightly sequenced. Each exercise was revised until testing showed that 90 per cent of the children could acquire a mean of 90 per cent of the specified behaviours of each exercise across the entire spectrum of test classrooms.

The basic assumptions underlying SAPA programme are:

- Science can be taught to young children in a way that is faithful to science as an intellectual approach to the world. For the SAPA programme, the primary implication is that children should learn, not so much the facts which are the outcome of scientific investigation, as the processes used by scientists. There are eight basic processes and five integrated processes contained in the programme.
- Science is best learned by doing science. Hands-on learning is the way to go.
- Lessons must take into account the empirical findings of developmental psychology. In SAPA, this assumption is treated in a pragmatic way. If a particular lesson cannot meet the 90-90 standard of mastery learning, analysis of the lesson may indicate that the cause may lie in a developmental problem. Revision and rewriting and retesting will fill up the deficiency. The SAPA programme uses the insights of the behaviour psychologist, Robert Gagne, as a functionary model in the programme design.

The process skills categorised by SAPA are:

Basic Processes

Table 2.1: Basic Process

Process	*Meaning*
Observing	using the five senses to gather information
Using Space/time Relationship	describing spatial relationships and their change with time
Classifying	imposing order on collections of objects or events
Using numbers	identifying quantitative relationships in nature
Measuring	measuring length, area, volume, weight, temperature, force and speed
Communicating	expressing ideas with oral and written words, diagrams, maps, graphs, mathematical equations and various kinds of visual demonstrations
Predicting	making specific forecast of what a future observation will be
Inferring	an explanation of an observation

Integrated Processes

Table 2.2: Integrated Process

Process	*Meaning*
Controlling variables	studying the influence of changing variables, the factors which influence one another
Interpreting data	using data to make inferences, predictions and hypotheses, the statistical treatments given to such interpretations and the study of probability
Formulating hypotheses	making generalized statements of explanations
Defining Operationally	defining terms in the context of experience
Experimenting	larger process of using basic and integrated processes

The process of investigation under SAPA begins in highly specific and concrete form and gradually generalizes by well-planned exercises. The processes are used as guidelines for constructing sequences of instruction. There is progressive development in each process category. As this development proceeds, the process turns to be increasingly interrelated, with corresponding development of other processes. Terminal behaviour is specified for each process, and the sequence of tasks that should be completed to develop the terminal behaviour is outlined in detail by means of task analysis. Thus we can summarise that the processes are carefully analysed in eight basic and five integrated processes.

Conceptually Oriented Programme in Elementary Science (COPES)

The Conceptually Oriented Programme in Elementary Science, popularly called COPES (1969), is was a science curriculum development project, centered on some of the major conceptual schemes in science. The project was undertaken by New York University and funded by the US Office of Education. The project grew out of a conference held in New York University in 1962. The participants, a wide ranging group of prominent scientists, educators, teachers and school administrators, felt that there was a need for a highly-structured, sequentially organized K-6 science programme.

After a long period of writing, field-testing, and rewriting, manuals suitable for wider implementation were published in 1971.

The basic assumptions underlying the COPES programme are programme were:

- The "best way to help young children attain a level of understanding and appreciation of science that will serve them through their adult lives ... is to focus their attention on certain "big ideas" in science, the broad, inclusive, conceptual schemes in terms of which the scientific community seeks to account for the familiar facts of nature ... all else in the science curriculum is related to these conceptual schemes."
- The second assumption is that children learn science best by doing science. There should be ample chance for hands-on learning. The COPES project provided no reading materials for children in order to guarantee that the materials themselves would be paramount.
- The third assumption is that the teaching and learning must take into account the experimental findings of developmental psychology. The lessons were carefully sequenced in the development of concepts. Pivotal concepts were introduced at progressively more complex levels from grade to grade. The COPES considered the following sequence of process as the basic skills:
    1. Analysing
    2. Classifying
    3. Communicating
    4. Experimenting
    5. Interpreting
    6. Mathematical reasoning
    7. Measuring
    8. Observing and

Minnesota Mathematics and Science Teaching Project (MINNEMAST)

Under the direction of James H. Werntz, Jr., Roger S. Jones, and

Wells Hively II at the University of Minnesota, this National Science Foundation supported programme was designed to be "the only elementary curriculum development project committed to designing a coordinated mathematics and science curriculum for the elementary schools." Based on the assumption, that thinking about math and science as distinct disciplines was not the best approach to building an elementary curriculum, the project attempted to exploit the relationship between the two disciplines".

Basic ideas behind this project are:

- The MINNEMAST materials attempt to teach "tools for life-long learning by emphasizing methods of acquiring knowledge rather than rote memorization of facts."
- Based on discovery learning principles, the activities are designed to lead the students to discover the intrinsic rewards of learning. Students do this by solving problems using both mathematical and scientific techniques that illustrate the larger processes of science and mathematics such as observation, generalization, experimentation, etc.
- Students are encouraged to watch and wonder, to classify and make qualitative comparisons such as greater than, less than, before, after etc. They learn the concept of one-to-one correspondence and pair objects in one set with those in another. As the students progress through the materials, they build upon these basic skills to learn basic math and science processes.
- From the very first activities, MINNEMAST materials work on the development of the child's natural curiosity, encouraging questions, to explore his or her environment, and to try to find answers to questions. One of the project's goals was to instil in the child, a lifelong interest in thinking and learning.

The principal aims stated in project literature about the MINNEMAST project literature are:

- To develop competency in both mathematics and science
- To provide experiences that involve the students in

challenging and interesting problem-solving situations, and,

- To provide settings that enable the children to explore, discover and clarify the relationship between mathematics and science wherever feasible.

Tennessee Science Curriculum Framework (TSCF)

The Tennessee Science Curriculum Framework, K-12 is was an attempt to change the way the Tennessee community of learners think about science. The community of learners includes students, families, educators, governmental organizations, business mens, industries, political leaders and all participants in the society. The framework promotes learning of science by doing science. It is a thoughtful response to a variety of reforms, beginning with the Tennessee Landmark Education Improvement Act (EIA) of 1992. This document has also incorporated ideas from the National Science Education Standards Project, American Association for Advancement of Science (AAAS), US Project 2061, National Science Teachers Association (NSTA) US and Scope Sequence and Coordination Project, as well as other state and national curriculum reform initiatives.

The framework was organized around four components: Process of Science of Science, Unifying Concepts of Science, Habits of Mind, and Science in Society. In each component, the generalized standards are written to accommodate a variety of instructional strategies and resources, yet they are pointed at specific concepts and skills that students should know and be able to do.

The objective of the document is to increase student's understanding of essential scientific concepts by promoting activities that engage students in doing science, using available technological tools, and rationally thinking about the natural world. To this end, the Tennessee Science Curriculum Framework, K-12 gives directions for an innovative approach to science education. It provides a philosophical foundation and a curricular framework from which educators may construct comprehensive science education programmes for elementary, middle, and high schools.

Tennessee's Four Components of Science Education

1. Process of Science

The process of science enables students to pose questions and investigate phenomena through language, methods, and instruments of science. Common science process themes include observing, questioning, collecting data, analyzing, explaining, and communicating. The process of science follows no single pathway but involves imagination, inventiveness, experimentation and logic, and evidence to support results. Once a question is posed, the search for answers follows a purposeful sequence of experimentation, data collection, analysis, and evaluation of conclusions, perhaps leading to new questions.

Technology provides tools and techniques that improve student's skills in measuring, calculating, recording, analyzing, modelling, and communicating. Hands-on explorations provide students with opportunities to use materials in new and concrete situations, to analyze results for greater understanding, to synthesize new ideas with what has been previously learned, and to evaluate how this new knowledge will be of practical use in their lives. Students may work in teams and share findings with others, but each individual should contribute to the group.

The Process of Science included in the frame work is listed below:

- Observing—the senses are used to develop an awareness of an event or object and the properties thereof.
- Questioning—the development of an inquisitive mind and the effective use of questioning techniques furthers the acquisition of information.
- Collecting data—the acquiring, recording, arranging and storing of information must be performed in a complete, accurate, concise, and user friendly manner.
- Analyzing—data should be examined to find patterns and relationships that may suggest cause and effect or support inferences and hypotheses.
- Explaining—phenomena and related information are made understandable through discussion that culminates in a higher level of learning.

- Communicating—an essential aspect of science is the act of accurately and effectively conveying oral, written, graphic or electronic information from the preparer to the user.

2. Unifying Concepts

Students acquire scientific knowledge by applying concepts, theories, principles and laws from life/environmental, physical and earth/space sciences. Any field of knowledge is more than an accumulation of isolated facts and ideas. In science, particularly, recurrent themes and concepts occur as our knowledge and understanding of the phenomena encountered in the natural world increases. Unifying themes connecting the science disciplines are scale and model, form and function, organization, interactions, change, and conservation. These themes provide the framework into which one can fit new discoveries and insights, thus making a complex field of knowledge more comprehensible and meaningful. Utilizing these themes to organize instruction in science, will ultimately provide students with a more coherent and integrated understanding of the World in which they live.

3. Habits of Mind

Students must be able to demonstrate ways of thinking and acting inherent in the practice of science and to exhibit an awareness of the historical and cultural contributions to the enterprise of science. Habits of mind include historical and cultural perspectives, assumptions, estimations and computations, scientific methods, an understanding of science and technology, and an appreciation of creative enterprises. Science is a creative process that attempts to discover and understand. Science questions all things and opens itself to continual scrutiny and modification. Science is carried out according to informed rules and assumptions. The rules and assumptions have developed over centuries from the experiences of those who have attempted to understand the natural world. However, as scientific knowledge grows, students should be prepared to alter their points of view. In this way, science is a never ending process of discovery, interpretation, and evaluation.

4. Science in Society

The student should be able to develop positive attitude towards science in solving problems and making personal decisions about issues affecting the individual, the society and the environment. Attitudes, personal needs, career goals, societal needs, economics, and politics all contribute to the role of science in society. Over the last several decades, the rate of scientific knowledge acquisition has increased dramatically. Fields such as medicine, space science, particle physics, and organic chemistry continue to produce information faster than it can be processed by any individual or group. The achievements in science and technology influence society, which either supports or limits the progress of science and technology. Therefore, the science curriculum should be structured to develop awareness of the interactions of science, technology, and society.

To meet these challenges presented by society, it is necessary for the science curriculum of our schools to address the attitudes, processes, tools, knowledge, and societal implications of science. This comprehensive approach to science education requires that learners receive essential readiness skills needed to become scientifically literate. Such skills go beyond learning; they give individuals a foundation for making sound decisions, understanding recent scientific advances and their implications, preparing to enter the job market, and developing a feeling of control over their lives.

Elementary Science Study (ESS)

ESS was an elementary school science programme that was supported primarily by grants from the National Science Foundation. The project began on a small scale in 1960. ESS Units were not explicitly tagged for the teaching of specific scientific concepts or aimed at a single grade level. The units were designed in such a way that they could be sequenced in a variety of ways. Structure was minimal. ESS units can be integrated into almost any science curriculum or combined to constitute a curriculum. Every unit was developed with the involvement of children and teachers. Testing was not so much concerned with cognitive outcomes as with motivation, curiosity, interest, involvement, and fun. If children are "turned on" by manipulating materials, experimenting, just messing about, then the unit was considered a success. Kits were produced for most units and the materials could often be "home made." There were no textbooks or student manuals, just a slim Teacher's Guide. Teacher training concentrated on giving teachers practice in joining their students as fellow investigators and acting as a resource group.

Basic Ideas: There are were several basic assumptions underlying the ESS programme—

- The first is was that science can be taught to young children in a way that is faithful to science as an intellectual approach to the world. In other words, the content must represent the best of scientific thinking in Physics, Chemistry, Biology, etc. The philosophy of the ESS group is was that the scientific principles should be taught more in an implicit manner than explicitly.
- The second assumption of the "new" science programme is was that children learn science best by doing science. Hands-on learning is the way to go. ESS takes the most radical approach to this principle by encouraging very open-ended activity with minimum of teacher direction.
- The third assumption is was that the lessons must take into account the empirical findings of developmental psychology. On this point ESS developers allow the children to function at their own levels; some will follow the activity on a very concrete level while others may go on to more abstract and formal thinking about what happens. This might vary widely within a classroom. The Harvard psychologist Jerome Bruner had a strong influence on the ESS programme.

Materials

The curriculum development process also involved commercial publishing houses, that helped with the development and packaging of classroom kits of materials. The logistics of supplying every teacher with all of the items necessary for each ESS unit proved to be a major challenge. The crucial problem turned out to be the ongoing maintenance of the items in the kits. Ultimately, school districts were successful in long term implementation of the programme if they faced this logistics problem by hiring a materials specialist. Another key to successful implementation was a team approach within each school that involved teachers and administrators.

Long Term Outcomes

ESS and other federally funded curriculum projects have continued to influence Elementary School Science instruction in a variety of ways. Commercial publishers have adapted large portions of the programmes into their current curriculum materials. Teachers today use many of the approaches pioneered in the NSF curricula. Many of the science educators preparing teachers in colleges and universities begin their own careers teaching these programmes in trial schools or work under educators who helped to develop or test the original programmes. Before the ESS group at Harvard and the other curriculum leaders did their work, science in the typical elementary school was a textbook subject and the content was a holdover from the nineteenth.

Elementary-School Science Project (ESSP)

Elementary-School Science Project attempts attempted to "foster the development of course materials that reflected a modern orientation to science and mathematics." The project was supported by the National Science Foundation, and the first book "Charting the Universe" was developed during the summer of 1961 by a group of astronomers and teachers who met at the University of Illinois under the direction of J. Myron Atkin and Stanley P. Wyatt at the University of Illinois, The Elementary-School Science Project was a precursor to curriculum projects that followed in that it attempted to develop scientific literacy in a bold new way. The materials in ESSP present a unique organization of elementary-school astronomy content, which was based on an identification of fundamental astronomical ideology. Embracing the interdisciplinary nature of astronomy, the activities in the project contains experiments based on science, history, geometry, and trigonometry. In doing so, it presents presented students with powerful methods of addressing the "big picture" ideas in science. Throughout the early and mid-sixties, the ESSP lessons and activities were tested by thousands of students in hundreds of classrooms.

ESSP attempts attempted to give students insight into what scientists do when scientists do science. The project strives strived to help students understand the intellectual activity astronomers undertake undertook as they gathered evidence and attempt to comprehend the structure of the systems of the universe.

The materials are was presented sequentially, with concepts being developed across the books of the series. In lessons filled with illustrations, historical references, tables, and graphs, the story of astronomy unfoldsunfolded. The dialogue leads readers down idea rich paths, often colliding into contradiction: "It soon becomes obvious that something is wrong." The astronomy lessons move from Einstein's ideas to molecular diagrams, from experiments with pennies to measuring the moon. Although the lessons contain a wide variety of activities, the number of fundamental.

Science Curriculum Improvement Study (SCIS)

The Science Curriculum Improvement Study is was a course content improvement project for grades K-8, which was funded by the National Science Foundation. Project headquarters was at the University of California, Berkeley. The project was the brainchild of Dr. Robert Karplus, a well known physics professor, at the Lawrence Livermore Laboratories at Berkeley. Professor Karplus, first became involved with the science education of young children when he attempted to help out at the elementary school attended by his own children. He soon realized that the task of providing young children with a solid foundation for scientific literacy required input from a variety of scientists and from developmental psychologists as well as experienced teachers and administrators. In the post-Sputnik era, science education was a major focus in the United States and the National Science Foundation had already funded major curriculum projects at the secondary school level.

There are several basic assumptions underlying the SCIS programme:

- The first is that science can be taught to young children in a way that is faithful to science as an intellectual approach to the world. In other words, the content must represent the best of scientific thinking in Physics, Chemistry, Biology, etc.

- The second assumption is that children learn science best by doing science. Hands-on learning is the way to go.
- The third assumption is that the lessons must take into account the empirical findings of developmental psychology. The SCIS programme used the findings of the psychologist, Jean Piaget, as a basis for the design of lessons. The lessons at all levels are characterized as 'exploration', 'invention' or 'discovery'. The lessons are intended to move children in the developmental sequence identified by Piaget: from the level of intuitive operations to concrete operations and then to formal operations.

Unified Science and Mathematics for Elementary Schools (USMES)

The project was based on an idea being promoted by many of today's educators, namely, that students could carry out long range investigations of real and practical problems based on their local environment. The project developed lessons containing examples of real life problem solving such as "Soft Drink Design" and "Burglar Alarm Design" as well as "Traffic Flow" and "Weather Predictions"

The USMES philosophy centers on the fact that multiple factors contribute to real-world problems. Solutions to such problems often involve interdisciplinary activities, and the problems found in USMES often involve overlap between natural sciences, social sciences, and mathematics. The problems posed by USMES activities are challenges, which may be handled at various levels of accomplishment by students across a wide range of grades. In fact, classes are encouraged to interpret the challenge, narrowing the statement of the problem to a specific one which they are able to operationalise. Students then enumerate the tasks to be done and decide on a specific course of action and delegation of responsibilities.

The content of USMES activities is are usually flexible enough to adapt to local discovery learning experiences. The students are encouraged to initiate the inquiry through activities based on the challenge. Through these activities, students investigate variables contributing to various aspects of the challenge. Challenges are complex, and may often be divided into several activities related to student interest and/or abilities. Collaboration is assumed, in both large and small groups. By focusing on the process of finding a solution, students begin to understand the power of scientific research, observation, data collection, and in-depth investigation.

USMES teachers gain a high degree of familiarity with the material, *possible* outcomes, discussions, observations, calculations, and constructions which may occur during the course of a challenge, which may take 60 to 70 hours, depending on the age of the children. Since children decide on the problem statement and may recommend multiple paths to solution, the actual outcomes, discussions, etc. are determined dynamically. The teacher becomes a motivator, facilitator, and resource on many levels. Sometimes one USMES challenge may lead to another and the work may flow spontaneously. Although this student-centered approach may seem intimidating to some teachers, the USMES programme provides a great deal of support for both teachers and students. Flow charts that outline possible scenarios for specific activities are given to teachers. "How-To" cards are designed to help students acquire specific skills or knowledge. Several examples are given which explain how USMES units worked in specific schools. The highly contextual, real-life nature of the USMES materials promote long term retention, and the project creators believed that one-fourth to one-third of the total school programme might be spent effectively on the interdisciplinary activities found in USMES. Both discovery learning and directed learning find a place in the USMES programme.

Science Curriculum (Elementary Catholic Schools) high lights the importance of process skills, by stating "Curriculum is designed to stimulate curiosity and to develop morally responsible, scientifically literate citizens". This curriculum stresses the process of science as a way of learning and further emphasizes that scientific knowledge is always subject to change based on additional knowledge. The processes of science are pictures as skills that are developing knowledge, concepts and application across the curriculum. The processes are often referred to as the "hands-on" approach to science and must be used throughout the programme. Each of the terms has been adapted from Elementary Science Studies, American Association for the Advancement of Science and Science Curriculum Improvement Studies, and implies active student participation. The objectives are, that all students will:

- develop an understanding of the processes and skills necessary for scientific investigation, problem solving, and critical thinking.
- develop responsible Christian decision making in matters related to science and technology's impact on society with respect for the environment and all living things.
- recognize that science is an integrated study that strongly involves religious beliefs, communication, mathematics, and technology.
- develop an interest, a sense of wonder, and curiosity about the study of the universe while recognizing the objective nature of science.
- develop an understanding of the scientific process and understand the structure of science, which includes organizing data into facts, principles, models, laws, and theories.
- realize the practical relationship of science to everyday life.

The science processes involved in this programme are:

- *Observing:* Using the senses to gather information about objects and events in the environment. This skill includes using scientific instruments to extend the range of the human senses and the ability to differentiate relevant from non-relevant.
- *Classifying*: A method for establishing order on collections of objects or events. Students use classification systems to identify objects or events, to show similarities, differences and interrelationships. It is important to realize that all classification systems are subjective and may change as criteria change. The test for a good classification system is whether others can use it or not.
- *Measuring:* A procedure for using instruments to determine the length, area, volume, mass or other physical properties

of an unknown quantity. It requires the proper use of instruments and the ability to calculate the measured results.

- *Using Numbers*: The skill includes: number sense, computation, estimation, spatial sense and whole number operation.
- *Communicating*: This is an important step for transmitting the results of observations and experimental procedures to others through the use of such devices as graphs, charts, tables, written descriptions, telecommunications, oral presentations, etc. Communication is fundamental to science, because it is in exchanging ideas and results of experiments that knowledge is validated by others.
- *Questioning:* The formulating of original questions based on observations and experiences with an event in such a way that one can experiment to seek the answers.
- *Relating:* In science, information about relationships can be descriptive or experimental. Relationships are based on logical arguments that encompass all data. Hypothetical reasoning, deductive reasoning, coordinate graphing, the managing of variables and the comparison of effects of one variable upon another contribute to understanding the "big" ideas of science.
- *Inferring:* An inference is a tentative explanation that is based on partial observations. Available data is gathered and an evaluation made based on the observed data. These judgments are never absolute and reflect what appears to be the most probable explanation at the time and are subject to change as new data are accumulated.
- *Predicting:* Using previously-observed information to make possible decisions about future events.
- *Formulating Hypothesis*: Stating a probable outcome for some occurrence based on many observations and interferences. The validity of the hypothesis is determined from testing of one or more experiments.
- *Identifying and Controlling Variables*: Determining what elements in a given investigation will vary or change and what will remain constant. Ideally scientists will attempt to identify all the variables before an investigation is conducted.

By manipulating one variable at a time they can determine how that variable will affect the outcome.

- *Experimenting*: The process is the culmination of all the science process skills. Experimentation often begins with observations, which lead to questions that need answers. The steps for proceeding may include forming a hypothesis, identifying and controlling variables, designing the procedure for conducting tests, implementing tests, collecting and interpreting the data and sometimes changing the hypothesis being tested.
- *Applying*: are applications of using knowledge to discover further information such as the process of inventing, creating, problem solving and determining probabilities.
- *Constructing Models*: are developing physical or mental representations to explain an idea, object or event. Models are usually developed on the basis of acceptable hypothesis.

Scientific Thinking (Scottish Education Department Curriculum)

The Scottish Education Department Consultative Committee (1969) elaborates one of its objectives as "acquisition of ability to solve problem situations and think scientifically." The committee further suggested the kinds of thinking which pupil will develop by studying science. They are enlisted in Table 2.3:

Nuffield Science Curriculum Project

Nuffield 11-13 (1986) distinguishes 'processes' and 'skills' listing as 'skills to be developed': handling equipment, observing, patterning, communicating, designing investigations and experiments, and mentally modelling. Notes on what is meant by 'patterning' indicate (Nuffield 11-13 (1986) Teachers' guide 1:17) that it includes classifying and predicting. 'Designing investigations' incorporates raising questions, hypothesizing and controlling variables. The skills to be developed in children according to the curriculum project Nuffield 11-13 are:

1. Handling equipment,

Table 2.3: Kinds of Thinking: The Scottish Education Department Consultative Committee (1969)

In Comprehending Knowledge	*In Application of Knowledge*	*In Analysis, Synthesis and Evaluation of Knowledge*
Observing Comparing Classifying Interpreting Discriminating Illustrating Extrapolating	Rearranging Relating Explaining Predicting Estimating	Justifying Assuming Inferring Imagining Inventing Discovering Generalizing Hypothesising Testing Reassessing Judging

2. Observing,
3. Patterning,
4. Communicating,
5. Designing investigations and experimentations, and
6. Mental modelling

Patterning includes classifying and predicting. Designing investigations incorporates raising questions, hypothesizing and controlling variables.

Warwick Science Process

In the curriculum project Warwick Science Process (Screen 1986), the following processes are were made explicit:

1. Observing,
2. Inferring,
3. Classifying,
4. Predicting,
5. Controlling variables, and
6. Hypothesizing

Assessment of Performance Unit (APU)

In the United Kingdom, the Assessment Performance Unit (APU) has established an assessment framework which identifies six Science Activity Categories (Murphy and Gott, 1984). They are listed below:

1. Use of graphical and symbolic representation,
2. Use of apparatus and measuring instrument,
3. Observation,
4. Application and interpretation of concepts and data,
5. Planning investigations, and
6. Carrying out investigations

Science in Process

'Science in Process' talks about the acquisition and use of process skills, and of processes being taught (ILEA, 1987). It draws attention to the following process skills:

1. Applying,
2. Interpreting,
3. Classifying,
4. Investigating,
5. Evaluating,
6. Observing,
7. Experimenting,
8. Predicting,
9. Hypothesizing,
10. Raising questions, and
11. Inferring

Conclusion

Despite the variations in terminology (processes, process skills, process outcomes, skills in science) there is obvious substantial common ground here. Many of the processes found due place in the list of curricula. This analysis reveals that the science processes are the pivot of almost all the science curriculum development around the world. And it continues in all the curricular revisions till present. This trend is spread over the realm of other subjects as processing of information. The corresponding skills are termed as information processing skills.

III

Scientific Method

The beginning of search for knowledge may be perhaps as old as human history. The problem solving ability in human beings began to emit with the dawn of intellect. The growth of science begins with man's observation of nature. He learned to make fire by using the scientific principle of friction, without knowing what or why of it. In his day-to-day life, he used many scientific principles for his livelihood without perfect understanding, but he has functional knowledge about them.

When we recall the evolution of science, we come to know that scientists of ancient and medieval times, with the exception of a few such as Archimedes and Hippocrates, adopted, adopted philosophical approaches in finding out solutions for their scientific problems. The earliest known roots of the scientific method has the existence as back as Imphotep—the original author of Edwin smith Papyrus (Circa 1600BC), the ancient surgical text book which reflects the basis components of scientific method: examination, diagnosis, treatment and prognosis. Ebers papyrus (Circa 1550 BC) also contains evidence of scientific empiricism. In ancient Greece, towards the beginning of the fourth century BC, some of the elements of the scientific thought were established. Greek philosophers believed in logic. Their insistence that people should produce evidence for their beliefs opened the way to modern science and philosophy. During the Hellenistic period, they made significant advancement in almost all the fields of science.

Aristotle (384-322 BC) turned away from theoretical philosophy to teach about practical ethics, self-control, logic, and science. He provided another crucial dimension to the scientific tradition by emphasizing empiricism. In Aristotelian science, we can find the beginning of primitive, inductive method which was based on collection of objects rather than experimentation. The adoption of pure scientific method in scientific investigation began only in the 17th century. Till that time, philosophical inquiries and scientific inquiries shaded into each other. The method of enquiry was more speculative than scientific. In investigations where the philosopher speculates on the entire field, the scientists remain close to the reality and do not attempt to pose impossible problems which he cannot answer. He The scientists poses problems pose problems in unambiguous and answerable forms in an unambiguous and answerable form. He then uses experimental method in his enquiries. Consequently science contains statements based on facts demonstrable, provable and verifiable by experiments. In solving problems, scientists use a combination of reasoning and experimentation, but philosophers use only reasoning. The scientific method originated from Philosophy and it has a philosophical background.

An excellent science teacher will train his or her students in scientific way of investigation for problem solving. To instil the spirit of scientific inquiry among students, is one of the major aims of science teaching. The prerequisite for training students in the method of science is the knowledge of scientific method, the skill to use it for solving problems and the right attitude towards it. An inquisitive, enthusiastic science teacher will inject the same qualities in his/her students. These students will be capable of using scientific method for finding solutions to the problems which they encounter in other fields of life. So the acquisition of knowledge and skill related to scientific method is very important in the training of a prospective science teacher.

Scientific Method and its Meaning

Scientific method means the method or procedure adopted by scientists in their investigation of natural phenomena, the way in which scientific generalizations are arrived at and made use of. It is a systematic and orderly method of solving problems. The problems of scientists usually arise out of the instincts of wonder and curiosity. Their aim is at bringing an event or phenomenon into an intelligent system into which it fits. A problem may arise in connection with the desire to meet a practical need. The scientists adopt a cautious and methodical procedure that helps them to acquire valid and verifiable conclusions. That methodical procedure need not be rigid and pre-planned. The method used in one inquiry may differ from others. They The scientists attack and solve their problems in various ways. But there are certain common elements or phases of procedure in all the scientific investigations. Scientific method refers to those common phases of procedure. Karl Pearson (1937) gave the method a definite form (Fig. 3.1). According to him, the method includes the following steps:

1. Sensing the problem,
2. Experimentation,
3. Collection of data, interpretation of data, and formulation of hypotheses,
4. Establishment of the law,
5. Generalization of the law,
6. Application of the law to new situations,
7. Predictability, and
8. Idealization and abstraction.

These steps can be broadly classified into two processes—

i. The Technical Process
ii. The Logical Process

The technical process comprises of experimentation, measurement and manipulation. The technical operations may vary in different fields of science. But the logical process of drawing conclusions is common to all sciences. The logical process is more important than technical process, because it is in the minds of scientists, the conclusions originate.

The logical process involved in the scientific method is in no way different from the thought process by which an ordinary person solves problems of daily life. The difference is only in the complexity

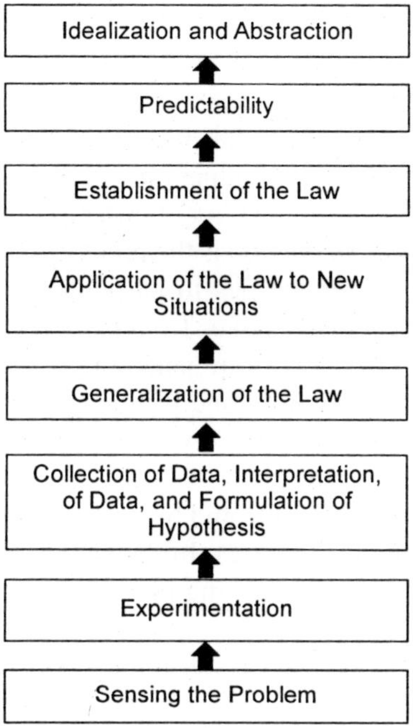

Fig. 3.1: The Scientific Method

and in the degree of perfection of the method of solution. Scientific method is only a refined form of critical thinking.

Therefore, a study of the method may be best done on the basis of the successive steps in the thought process. A complete act of thought may be analysed in the following steps:

- A felt difficulty.
- Its location and definition.
- Suggestion of probable solutions.
- Finding out the bearing of the suggestion of the solution by employing reasoning.
- Further observation and experimentation leading to its acceptance or rejection.

Thus Scientific method is an expansion of required thought process.

Some Elements of Scientific Method

Drawing Inference

Scientific method primarily makes use of two types of reasoning in drawing inferences. They are induction and deduction. *Induction* is the process of arriving at some kind of order or regularity among the phenomena observed. *Deduction* is the process of applying inductive conclusions, laws, or regularities to particular cases. In induction, the mind of the investigator moves from particular to general, while in deduction, the thinking is from general to particular. Induction is the method of finding out laws and principles and deduction is that of applying them. In scientific investigation, both induction and deduction are made use of.

Deduction: It was Aristotle and his followers introduced the use of deductive reasoning (Fig. 3.2). In deduction, one proceeds from general to specific statements using prescribed rules of logic. It is a system for organizing known facts in order to reach a conclusion. It operates through a series of statements known as syllogisms containing.

a) the major premise or statements on reasoning is based.
b) the minor premise.
c) the conclusion.

For Example:

(a) Metals expand on heating (major premise)
(b) Aluminium is a metal (minor premise)
(c) Therefore aluminium expands on heating (conclusion)

Scientific inquiry cannot be conducted through deductive reasoning alone because of the difficulty involved in establishing the universal truth of many statements concerning scientific phenomena. But deductive reasoning is useful as it provides a means for linking theory and observations. It helps the researcher to deduce from existing theory what phenomena to be observed. Deductions from theory provide hypotheses.

Fig 3.2: Deductive Reasoning

Induction: It was Francis Bacon, that, that advocated this type of reasoning. He held the view that thinkers should not enslave themselves by accepting premises handed down by authority as absolute truth. He emphasised that an investigator should establish general conclusion on the basis of facts gathered through observation. He insisted that for obtaining knowledge, one should observe nature, gather particular facts, and formulate generalisations. This approach is known as inductive reasoning which is the reverse process employed in the deductive approach.

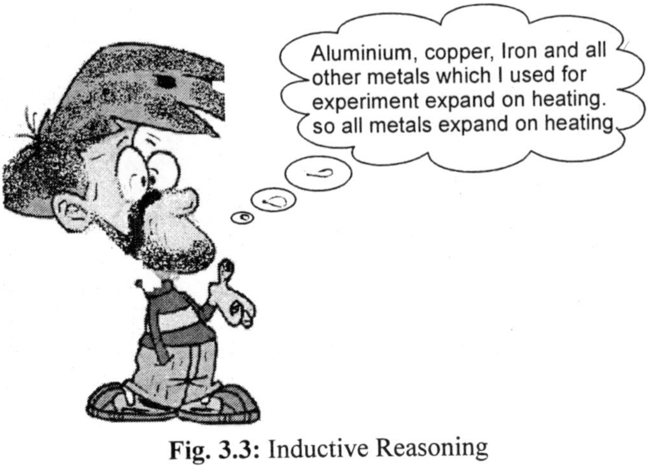

Fig. 3.3: Inductive Reasoning

All inductive inferences are based on the following assumptions:

1. The law of uniformity of nature: i.e. a phenomenon that has taken place under certain circumstances will repeat itself whenever the same circumstances occur.
2. The law of causation: i.e. every phenomenon has a cause or set of causes that is invariably connected with it.

Mill's Canons of Induction

In some circumstances, it is not possible to isolate the operating cause from the other experimental conditions. In complex cases, the effects and causes may remain conjoined, or if there is plurality of causes, it is difficult to decide which is the cause and which is the effect. In such cases, we might try to establish the causal relation by adopting one of the following methods known as Mill's canons of induction. The general principle underlying the canons may be stated as "If other things remaining essentially the same, a certain factor or circumstance cannot be omitted or quantitatively changed, without changing a certain phenomenon, that factor or circumstance is the cause of that phenomenon".

The investigator should examine a large number of instances of the phenomenon in question, under sufficiently varied circumstances to enable us to detect the cause and the effect. The following are the canons:

- The method of agreement
- The method of difference
- The joint method
- The method of residues
- The method of concomitant variations

The Method of Agreement

If in every observed instances of a phenomenon, only one circumstance is common that circumstance is probably a cause or condition of phenomenon.

Symbolically:

$$\frac{abcd....}{pqrs....} : \frac{bcef....}{qrts....} : \frac{cefg....}{xpry....}; \textit{ therefore } \frac{c}{r}$$

e.g. 1. We compare different substances, which exhibit the phenomenon of efflorescence, but have no other point of agreement. If in all these cases, we find that the substances contain water of crystallization and that there are no other common circumstances, we may legitimately conclude that presence of water of crystallization is a cause of efflorescence.

e.g. 2. If dew is found deposited on a number of surfaces which are different in all respects except in that they are all at a lower temperature than the surrounding atmosphere. Then the lower temperature is a condition of the deposition of the dew.

The conclusions obtained by this method are not decisive. Unless a good number of varied circumstances are considered, and all casual circumstance eliminated, the method may lead to absurd inferences. There is also a practical difficulty of finding out common circumstances in a large number of antecedents. Want of adequate analysis of complex circumstances and the consequent omission to take note of all relevant conditions are also causes of failure.

The method of agreement, though not fool-proof, may with proper caution, be made use for suggesting a clue to be followed by other methods.

The Method of Difference

Whenever the elimination of a single circumstance is accompanied by the non-occurrence of a phenomenon that circumstance is probably related to its causation.

Symbolically:

Positive instance Negative instance

$$\frac{abcd}{pqrs} \qquad \frac{abc}{pqr} \quad \text{Therefore, } \frac{d}{s}$$

Examples:

1) If a surface exposed to air is dry at the atmospheric

temperature and it become wet on lowering its temperature, other conditions remaining unaltered, we might reasonably conclude that lowering of temperature is the cause of wetness.

2) A musical note is produced when the violin string vibrates. But when the vibrations are stopped, other conditions being the same, the note ceases to be produced. Hence we infer that the vibrations of the string are causally connected to the note.

In this method, we compare two instances—one in which the phenomenon occurs and the other in which it does not occur. What is most important is that they should differ only in one relevant circumstance. The two instances may be two successive stages of the same relevant circumstance differing only by one antecedent and one consequent. Or they might be two independent and separate instances. But it is rare that we meet such instances in nature. Hence this requirement should be arranged experimentally, taking care that no more than one circumstance is varied at a time. Under such conditions, the method yields good results.

The Joint Method

The joint method states that, If in one group of cases in which a phenomenon occurs, there is one and only one common circumstance, while in another group of cases, in which the phenomenon does not occur and there is nothing in common, except the absence of the above circumstance, then the phenomenon is causally related to that circumstance.

This is a combination of the method of agreement and difference. The suggestion of causation arrived at by the method of agreement is strengthened by the method of difference. The application of this method leads to fairly valid conclusions.

The Method of Residues

The Method of Residues states that "if part of a complex phenomenon is known to be causally related to certain operating circumstance, the residual part of the phenomenon must be due to the rest of the relevant circumstance (known or unknown)".

This method suggests how we might obtain a complete knowledge of a complex phenomenon, part of which is already accounted for by its known causal relationship with certain circumstances. Obviously the unexplained residual part of the phenomenon must be due to the causes which may or may not known to exist. The observation of the residual effects leads to the search for the antecedent.

It must be noted that the method does not necessarily help us to determine the cause of the residual phenomenon, but it limits the field of enquiry and makes it easier to hit on a suitable hypothesis.

Example 1: The orbit of Uranus as observed by astronomers was found to be slightly different from its nature as calculated on the basis of the law of gravitation, even though the influence of all the known planets were taken into account. The residual influence was therefore surmised to be due to the effect of some unknown planet. The extent of the deviation of orbit of the planet, and its direction were calculated and actual observation in the calculated direction led to the discovery of planet Neptune.

Example 2: The residual density of atmospheric nitrogen in comparison with pure chemical nitrogen led to the discovery of argon.

The Method of Concomitant Variations

The Method of Concomitant variations states that "if two phenomena vary concomitantly, while all other relevant circumstances remain unchanged, they must be causally related".

Symbolically:

$$\frac{Abcd_1....}{Pqrs_1....} \quad \frac{Abcd_2....}{Pqrs_2....} \quad \frac{Abcd_3....}{Pqrs_3....} \quad Therefore\ \frac{d}{s}$$

As the method implies a quantitative variation of the antecedent produces a quantitative variation of the consequent, it is helpful in establishing quantitative correlations between causally connected phenomena (quantitative induction). This is the most important method employed in science. The validity of such quantitative laws depends on the degree of accuracy with which the varying phenomena are measured. These laws are applicable only with in the limits between which the phenomena have been varied experimentally.

The concomitant variation may be of two types; direct or inverse. When the antecedent and consequent increase or decrease together it is said to be direct. When one of them increases as the other decreases, the variation is inverse.

e.g. Gravitational force between two bodies varies directly with their masses and inversely with the square of the distance between them.

e.g. 1: The change of volume of a gas is observed to be accompanied by a change of temperature and pressure. To decide which of them is the cause or whether both of them are independent causes, each of them should be kept constant and the other vary. The observations thus made reveal the concomitant variation of pressure, volume and temperature. Thus we conclude that both pressure and volume are causally related to temperature. Accurate measurement of variations of pressure and volume (while temperature kept constant) and mathematical calculations based on them leads to Boyle's law. Similarly the variation in change in temperature and volume (pressure being kept constant) leads up to Charles's law.

Table 3.1: Mill's Canons of Induction

Canon	*Context*	*Inductive Reasoning*
The method of agreement	All possible instances of a phenomenon are observed. In all the instances only one common circumstance is found.	The common circumstance present in all the instances is the cause of the phenomenon.
The method of difference	Two instances are compared. In first, the phenomenon occurs. In the second, the phenomenon does not occur. The two instances are differed in only one circumstance.	The differing circumstance is probably the cause of the phenomenon
The joint method	Two groups of instances are compared. In one group, the phenomenon occurs. In the second group, the phenomenon does not occur. The groups are differing in only one circumstance.	The differing circumstance is probably the cause of the phenomenon

(*Contd.*)

Canon	*Context*	*Inductive Reasoning*
The method of residues	A phenomenon has two parts. The cause of one part is known.	The residual part of the phenomenon must be due to the rest of the relevant circumstance (known or unknown)
The method of concomitant variations	Two phenomena vary concomitantly, while all other relevant circumstances remain unchanged.	Then the two phenomena must be causally related

The above method of induction suggested by Mill should not be considered as infallible. They cannot be invariably suggested causal relations. Difficulty arises when there is a plurality of causes for the same effect or when different effects remain mixed up. It may be pointed out that the method is applicable only to causes that can be perceived by the senses. They cannot be applied to the more hidden laws, which really express the most fundamental laws of the nature.

Analogy

Scientific method makes use of analogy also in drawing inferences in scientific investigations. Analogy is the most primitive type of inference. Whenever we perceive a new object or event the first impulse of our mind is to compare and connect it with the nearly similar previous experiences. When two objects or phenomena are similar in some respects, we anticipate that these will be similar in some other aspects also. Analogical type of reasoning is helpful in understanding new experiences and suggesting causal relations.

In science, analogy has played an important role in the field of discovery. The wave theory of sound is suggested by the ripples on the surface of water and wave theory of light by the propagation of sound waves through air. The heliocentric theory of solar system has its support from the analogy of the miniature planetary system of Jupiter and its satellites.

The conclusions drawn by analogical reasoning are much less reliable than those of induction because, no invariable connection is established between the antecedent and the consequent. The validity of conclusions drawn depends not on the number of similarities but on the depth of the similarities. Very often it may happen that the similarities may be only apparent and superficial. In such cases, we

Fig. 3.4: Analogy

are likely to be misleading by analogy. Hence analogy should be handled with great caution.

Analysis and Synthesis

Analysis and synthesis form the real foundation of the scientific method. Analysis means separating into parts and synthesis means putting together. Inference is possible only through the mental process of analysis and synthesis. In induction, we analyze the various facts into its components, and synthesise them to formulate relationships.

Fig. 3.5: Analysis of a Problem

Natural phenomena are mostly complex in their conditions. We have to analyse them into their components in order to find the cause effect relationships. Progress in science depends on this ability to separate ideas into its components. Analysis is facilitated by comparison of different objects or phenomena which are similar in some respects.

Having analyzed a phenomenon, we have to synthesise its components in different ways, there by we can formulate definitions and causal relations or laws. Analysis and synthesis are particularly important in the study of a phenomenon having plurality of causes. The effect of each cause acting separately may study in turn and the total effect may be estimated by the process of synthesis.

e.g.: Compounds may be split up into elements and elements may be combined to form compounds. Cavendish proved that water is a compound of hydrogen and oxygen by the process of synthesis. Davy proved that water can be split up into hydrogen and oxygen by the process of analysis. Both analysis and synthesis are necessary for a complete scientific treatment.

Hypothesis

Hypothesis is an intelligent shrewd guess or inference that is formulated and provisionally adopted to explain observed facts or phenomenon. It is the most suitable solution for a problem at hand. It plays an important role in scientific investigation. Critical examination of facts and its purposeful reflection lead to suggestion of tentative solution (hypothesis).

Sources of Hypotheses: Analogy and simple methods of induction are helpful in formulating hypotheses. Breadth of knowledge and imaginative insight of the investigator will help much in this regard. For this, the investigator should have wide reading, familiarity with the existing practices and first hand contact with the pertinent data. Discussions, lecturing about the problem, and constructing models relating to the problem etc. will help the formulation of hypothesis. In general, it may be said that hypothesis occur to a mind that are prepared to interpret facts.

Fig. 3.6: The Act of Hypothesising

Purpose of Hypothesis

The following are the purposes of hypothesis:

- It provides a tentative explanation of the phenomenon.
- It provides the investigator with a relational statement that is directly testable in an investigation.
- It provides direction to research.
- It provides a framework for reporting the conclusions of the investigation.

Criteria of Good Hypothesis

The following are the criteria of a good hypothesis:

- It must have an explanatory power.
- It must be consistent with universal laws which have been established beyond doubt.
- It should be simple. It should be stated clearly and precisely in unambiguous terms.
- It should be testable.
- It should be adequate enough to explain the observed facts.
- It should state the expected relationship between variables.
- It should be limited in scope.

Types of Hypotheses

Hypotheses are classified as directional hypotheses and non-directional hypotheses.

Directional Hypotheses: The hypotheses, which stipulate the direction of the expected differences or relationships, are termed as directional hypotheses.

e.g. "There will be a positive relationship between individual's attitude towards high caste Hindus and his socio-economic status."

Non-directional Hypotheses: It is a research hypothesis, which does not specify the direction of expected differences or relationships is a non-directional hypothesis.

e.g. There is no significant difference in the means of scores on self esteem of boys and girls in upper primary schools of Kottayam district.

A research hypothesis can take either declarative form, the *null* form or *question* form. When the researcher makes a positive statement about the outcome of the study, the hypothesis takes the declarative form. e.g. 'The means of scores on academic achievement of extroverts is significantly higher than that of introverts', is stated in the declarative form. In such statements, the researcher makes a prediction based on his theoretical formulations of what should happen if the explanations of the behaviour he has given in his theory are correct.

In the null form, the researcher makes a statement that no relationship/difference exists. The hypothesis, that 'There exists no significant difference between the means of scores on academic achievement of high school athletes and that of non-athletes' is an example of null hypothesis. Since null hypotheses can be tested statistically, they are often known as statistical hypotheses. They are also known as testing hypotheses when declarative hypotheses are tested statistically by converting it into null form.

In the question form hypothesis, a question is asked as to what the outcome will be, instead of stating what outcome is expected. e.g. Will teaching children through programmed instruction decrease their test anxiety.

Testing of Hypothesis: After the problem has been solved, the conclusion arrived at must be validated. This is an important step in the scientific method. Here defects in the data or error in the reasoning process may lead to faulty conclusion. Hence a conclusion has to be tested for its validity. The awareness regarding the need for testing conclusions and the habit of open mindedness must develop in pupils, which are essential for scientific investigation. Several hypotheses may have to be discarded on the basis of tests, observations and experiments, new hypotheses may be formulated and tested till one hypothesis is proved to be valid.

Collection of Facts and Data

Facts are necessary to help us to form and test hypotheses. Data collection is an important part of any scientific study. Collection of data relating to the problem at hand is the starting point of any scientific investigation. Facts form the bricks with which we construct the edifice of science. All knowledge is primarily derived from such experiences, which we call facts. Facts help us to frame hypotheses. So it is important that facts collected should be accurate comprehensive and impersonal. The validity of scientific conclusion ultimately depends on careful collection of facts. After collecting the relevant facts by observation (natural observation) and experiment (artificial observation), these are used to draw logical conclusions using the reasoning process.

Observation

Observation is the process of data collection by using the senses. It is the prolonged perception of things or events directed and sustained by attention. It is the sole process by which we collect facts. It consists in collecting facts, which are in direct knowledge of the investigator. Observation is perception with a purpose. In observation, only the relevant things are taken into account. Therefore it is essentially selective. Observation is not the same as inference. Observation is the knowledge directly gained through sense organs. But inference is the process of passing from a known proposition to an unknown or implied proposition. Thus inference is indirect knowledge where as observation is direct knowledge.

Components of Observation

Observation has three components—sensation, attention and

perception. Sensation is derived from the sense organs. The accuracy of observation depends to a great extent on the power of the sensory organs. Attention is related to the ability to concentrate up on the object matter of study. Perception enables the mind to reorganize the facts by identifying sensations and drawing up on experience and introspection.

Observation may sometimes take place unintentionally or accidentally. In some cases, such casual observation leads to the discovery of great scientific principles or laws. Even though, observation in scientific investigation must be purposeful, indiscriminate observation of everything without any purpose is a waste. Since inferences and judgments form an inevitable part of observation, it is important that the observer should be free from prejudice or bias. Successful observation can only be made on the basis of pertinent previous knowledge, which enables an observer to select and isolate important features of observation. Not only our senses but instruments like telescope and microscope, which we use as aids to our senses, have their limits and the results of observation are necessarily bound by them.

Experiment

When observation is arranged and controlled, it becomes artificial. Actually, the artificial observation is called experiment. Experiment is an active observation where we study phenomena under purposively pre-arranged conditions. Systematic variations of the conditions make it easier to eliminate the irrelevant conditions and to determine the exact causal relationship between connected circumstances. The acquisition of a large part of our scientific knowledge has been made possible by the experimental process of inquiry. Experience and insight are necessary to disregard the obviously irrelevant conditions and confine our attention to those that may probably have an influence on the phenomenon under study. After choosing the relevant conditions we must vary one condition at a time, maintaining all the others unchanged. If we vary more than one condition at a time, we cannot decide which of the varied conditions is, the cause of the observed effect. If two conditions are varied at a time, the effect of one may have neutralized the effect of the other. A single omission of a relevant condition often leads to erroneous results. So all the relevant conditions should be varied one at a time and their effects should be studied individually.

Characteristics of Experiment

An experiment has three characteristics:

i. An independent variable which is manipulated.
ii. Controlled variables i.e. all other variables except the independent variable which is held constant.
iii. The dependent variable on which the effect of the independent variable is observed.

Limitations of Experiment

The following are the limitations of experiment:

i. Experiment is not always possible (e.g. astronomical phenomena, formation of rock, evolution of species etc.)
ii. Variation of one condition at a time is not always possible. In most of the cases the conditions are interdependent.
iii. Some conditions such as gravitation, friction and heat are incapable of elimination and some other variables are incapable of elimination within certain limits.
iv. At times we are led to wrong conclusions on account of unsuspected conditions influencing the result. Then it is by sheer chance that truth is revealed.

Advantages of Observation over Experiment

i. Experiment is not possible in all cases. But observation can be carried out for all possible cases. Experiment is sometimes impossible or dangerous, but observation is not so. The scope of observation is much wider than that of experiment.
ii. The preparation for experiment is depended upon observation. Prior observation is a condition for experiment. Observation may go without experiment, but experiment cannot go without observation.
iii. In observation, we can have reason and argument from cause to effect, and from effect to cause. That is, argument may be

forward or backward. But in experiment, it is not so. Experiment proceeds from cause to effect. In observation, thus, we can find out the cause of the effect or the effect of the cause; but experiment only unfolds the effect, the cause being given.

Advantages of Experiment over Observation

i. In experiment, it is possible to isolate the factors involved in a phenomenon. But in simple observation, it cannot be done. This can be done by making one factor variable and the others constant. In simple observation, since the conditions are not controlled, factors cannot be varied and made constant systematically.
ii. In experiment, we can easily reproduce the phenomenon and vary the circumstances indefinitely. But in observation, we have to depend up on nature for the supply of appropriate instances. In experiment, we may have as many instances as possible. But in experiment we have to wait for the mercy of nature for a favourable circumstance.
iii. Since, the circumstances are within our control in an experiment, things can be examined with sufficient calmness and care. But in simple observation, we may have to be haste, as the phenomenon may disappear quickly. The observer has to wait, but nature does not, in simple observation.

Authority and Testimony

It is quite natural that one seeks answers to the questions from some one who has experience with the problem or has some other sources of expertise. From time immemorial, man has been doing this. Authority and testimony are two such sources of knowledge.

Testimony means personal or documentary evidence or attestation in support of a statement or fact. Authority refers to the right to command or give an ultimate decision. We often accept as truth the word of those who are recognized as authorities. "*To know the population we depend on the census report*". "*A student will refer Daniel John's pronouncing dictionary to know the correct pronunciation.*"

As sources of truth, authority and testimony have several drawbacks. They can be wrong. They have no claim of infallibility. More over, they are often based on personal opinions rather than facts. Scientific method seldom makes use of authority and testimony for drawing inference.

Scientific Method and Transfer of Training

The value of training involved in scientific method is realized only when such training is carried over to other fields of life. But studies in transfer of training show that, transfer is not automatic and cannot be secured unless the teacher knows the conditions and methods of effective transfer.

Tips to Ensure Transfer of Training

1. The subject matter and methods chosen for instruction should be useful and common in day-to-day life situations of pupils.
2. Whenever possible, the subject matter should be presented to children through problems which are within the range of their interest and needs, of their knowledge and of their powers of abstraction.
3. The students should be shown that the method used to solve each type of problem is applicable to numerous other problems of everyday life.
4. The students should be shown the successful application of the method of great scientists, so that they might be inspired by ideals of methodical procedure. These ideals will be carried over in all their activities.

Application of Scientific Method to the Teaching of Science

Physics and Chemistry being highly developed branches of science are best suited for developing the scientific method of thinking in children. Training in scientific method is advocated because; such rational thinking is indispensable to everyone for the successful solution of the various problems of life. The differences between scientific thinking and everyday thinking are one of the degrees of perfection. The man of science uses with exactness the methods, which the common man uses carelessly in his everyday life.

Let every science teacher begin his/her class with by presenting genuine presenting genuine problem in which his pupils are interested. Let him help the students to recognize new and challenging problems by setting up suitable situations. Unless the students sense the problem as their own, they cannot be expected to perform the mental processes needed for their solutions. The teacher should stimulate and guide them in the thought process. He should guide them to choose the best method of procedure. They must be made to realize the advantage of methodical procedure so that they might become inspired by its idea.

Conclusion

The application of scientific method gives students the training in science process skills as every step in a scientific inquiry resembles process skills. Though some are arguing that there is no particular method for conducting scientific inquiry since different problems at different contexts needs particular operations. These different operations include scientists' actions, which may be a basic skill like observation or an integrated skill like experiment. Therefore, a judicious use of scientific method for teaching suitable topics will lead the children and the science instructions to the desirable end.

IV

Science Process Skills

Development of science has been the result of man's inquiry of puzzling natural phenomena and situations with a view to satisfy his innate curiosity and to subdue the environment for enhancing his physical comforts. For this purpose, he built builds up a body of scientific knowledge by utilizing his intellect and applying his ability for engaging in thinking and reasoning. This shows that even in ancient times science was really the product of precise method of thinking rather than mere acquisition of readymade facts. But when the body of scientific knowledge expanded, the spirit of inquiry gave way to mere information mongering in the hands of incompetent teachers. The unscientific system of examination, calling for mere reproduction of this information, added momentum to this degeneration. Thus, the true spirit of science which is built upon the real process and thinking and learning was lost sight of.

The vital role of science education is to help students develop the thinking skills of scientists. During 1960's, the focus of science education research, centered up on designing curricula that promote scientific inquiry by allowing students to undertake scientific investigations. Many science programmes were developed to promote reasoning skills scientists used in their investigations among students.

Emergence of Science as a Process

The emergence of science as a process overthrew the older concept of science as a lump of content to be taught and learnt for examination purposes. It is in the late decades of 20th century that the 'process' element began to acquire prominence in science teaching. The major shift in emphasis is attributed to two major factors.

(i) As a reaction against fact-laden, content oriented science teaching and information based encyclopaedic science textbooks that pervaded science teaching at different stages.

(ii) The works of prominent educational thinker like John Dewey and the pragmatic school of educational philosophy which helped to direct the educational activity towards experiences as the basis of education, and the advance to the stress on scientific method.

The influence of Dewey on modern education needs very little highlighting. Much of what he preached has been carried into modern educational practice. Dewey equated purposeful thought with scientific processes. Many modern curriculum designers attempted to translate Dewey's ideas into educational practice, developed curriculum designs with stress on the teaching of science as 'problem solving' or 'process' because they wanted to develop children's thinking ability (Joyce, *et al.* 1970).

Significance of Process Skills in Science Teaching

In many countries, attempts have been made to reorient the curriculum so as to give due importance to processes in science education. The major goals of these curricular innovations can be classified as:

i. The development of curricular materials and science programme that are consistent with current science knowledge.
ii. The development of curricular materials and science programmes which provide the student with an understanding of the processes of science (AAAS, 1994).

Donnely (1985) suggests the conditions for having a practical theoretical role for science processes in science curricula and its implementation. They are:

i. The processes must be defined at some minimum level of coherence.

ii. Their connection if any, with pupil's intellectual skills must be ascertained.
iii. Methods for the development of the relevant skills must be explored.

National committee on science education standards and assessment (1994 draft) advanced inquiry as an important standard for grades 9 to 12. Enquiry in the classroom is a means for promoting and supporting students' curiosity and questioning spirit. Inquiry is a critical component of the science curriculum at all grade levels and in every domain of science.

It serves four essential functions:

i. To assist in the development of an understanding of scientific concepts.
ii. To develop an understanding of the nature of scientific inquiry.
iii. To develop the skills and the disposition to use them necessary to become independent inquirers about the natural world.
iv. As a model of how we know and what we know in science.

The science criteria framed by the evaluation system of General Certificate of Secondary Education (GCSE1986) also emphasizes the development of skills. They are enlisted below:

i. The relative weight given to skills and methods must increase.
ii. The relative weight given to facts and terminology must decrease.
iii. Experimental work must be included.
iv. Everyday life and socio-economic implications of science must be considered (Cooper, 1986).

Bruner (1962) insists that the memorization of facts is not as important as the acquisition of process of knowledge. "To instruct some someone in a discipline is not a matter getting him to commit results to mind. Rather it is to teach him to participate in the process that makes possible the establishment of knowledge. We teach a subject not to produce little living libraries on the subject, but, rather to get a student to take part in the process of knowledge. Getting knowledge is a process, not a product."

Some science educators (Simpson, 1987) raise strong arguments for a process-led science curriculum. They question the relevance of teaching of facts in the situation where information is generated in gigantic amount. Learning and education do not involve the passive handling and acquisition of information. Human beings are information processors, rather than information absorbers and active learning involves the processing of new information according to learner's previous experiences, needs, preconceived ideas, knowledge, and hypotheses. So in addition to the information skills, previous ideas, experiences, and hypotheses should present in the learner's cognitive structure.

Willington (1990) substantiates that science education should focus on the following equally:

i. Knowledge 'that'—facts, happenings and phenomena.
ii. Knowledge 'how'—skills, processes and abilities.
iii. Knowledge 'why'—explanations, models, analogies, theories etc.

The transferable skills deserve the position of basis for science education than the facts, which soon get outdated. Therefore outdated. Therefore, science education should aim at develop the transferable skills.

A critical view on the major curricular innovations reveals that, when processes and attitudes are considered as the main focus, the role of specific content is generally played down. This deals to an inductive view of learning science. The generalizations formulated by using the process skills add to the children's conceptual knowledge of the world around them.

The alternative school of thought regards the teaching of concepts as significant for children's understanding of the environment. Even though they use process skills during teaching and learning, the focus is on product. The underlying approach to learning is deductive. Children learn the generalizations, and then they will use them in understanding things around.

For effective teaching and learning of science, a learning approach in which the processes and products are needed rather than the process-product polarization. Modern educators are of the opinion that content of an activity influences children's use of process skills. Any activity will have some content, which influence the thinking and exploration.

The process approach has many sided significance numerous benefits. It stimulates autonomous recognition of relationships, broadens background knowledge for current and future use, reinforces the skills and motivates the pupil towards self education.

The National Council of Educational Research and Training (NCERT) while planning the integrated curriculum for middle schools students identified the process approach as one of the core elements of the course. While discussing the philosophy of the integrated curriculum—an introduction (NCERT, 1982) states, "....a science curriculum must stress more on.....the processes than the products of science. The knowledge of the product is useful in understanding the processes of science and for concretizing the processes for pedagogical use. But understanding of the processes is useful both for daily life as well as in furthering scientific knowledge.

Definition of Process Outcomes

The term process outcomes has been used with slightly different connotations by specialists in the area, despite the fact that there is considerable overlap among the theoretical conceptualisation of the basic term and its allied terms. But the allied terms like "processes", "mental processes", "cognitive processes", "scientific processes" etc.; have also been brought under discussions.

Process: A process is a series of activities or operations performed to attain certain goal or product. Horrace (1985) defines a process as: 1) the manner in which a change is affected specifically a change in response strength as a result of a particular experimental operation. 2) A process may involve mental activities like perceiving, thinking, feeling or acting. Oxford dictionary (1968) defines a process as a continuous or regular action or succession of actions taking place or carried on a definite manner. The meaning of the term "process" varies in different epistemological contexts. In certain contexts, it stands for a series of thinking processes, which together stand for a major stage with in a system of processes that lead to generation of new knowledge. The term as applied to science, stands for a group of activities and thought processes that define a major stage in a scientific investigation (Suresh, 1991).

Mental Process: Russel defines a thought process as awareness of meaning and of relation and consciousness of rule and intention (Bloom, 1969). Wolman (1973) defines mental process as the action of an organism which involves the mind.

Cognitive Process: The term cognitive process is used by in ERIC (1982) as synonymous with "thinking process". According to this group, a cognitive process stands for the process based on perception or memory through which an individual obtains knowledge or conceptual understanding. e.g., perceiving, judging, abstracting, reasoning, imagining, remembering, and anticipating. Modern educational and psychological literature prefers the word "cognitive processes" to the word "thought process".

Scientific Process: Nay *et al.* (1971) defines a scientific process as "a series of activities or operations performed by the scientist in his attempt to understand nature. A scientific inquiry means a systematic and investigative performance which incorporates inductive thinking capabilities after a person has acquired a broad and critical knowledge of the particular subject matter through formal reasoning process.

Outcome: the word "outcome" is used to stand for something that is achieved at the end of planned series of activities. Good (1973) defines an (educational) outcome as change in behaviour resulting from learning. Outcomes of education, used in this sense, are the result of consequences of education, made explicit in the form of behavioural changes. This is different from the term "objective". An objective is nothing but a desired result.

Process Outcomes in Science: The term "process outcomes" as applied to science stands for the intellectual skills needed for scientific investigations attained by the student as a result or consequence of learning science. The intellectual skills stand for the skills required for completing a stage or stages of a focused scientific investigation. (Suresh,1991).

Science processes are the inter linked activities performed by any qualified person during the exploration of universe. The science process outcomes are the intellectual skills needed for scientific investigation attained by students as a result of learning of science.

Process vs Product Approach

The body of scientific knowledge, which is the result of the quest for comprehension and explanation through the development of fundamental principles is called the 'content' or 'products' or 'major concepts' of science.

The body of knowledge may be seen as a collection of knots. When the little knots are tied in the bigger ones, making generalizations, science begins to make sense. The method used by scientists for acquiring the body of knowledge is known as the scientific method or method of inquiry or processes of science. The scientists use experimentation and observation as basis for developing conceptual schemes. The development of conceptual schemes by experiment and observation and the premise that these conceptual schemes lead to further experimentation and observation are considered as the fundamental aspects of the nature of science. The cyclic nature of the genesis of conceptual schemes from observation and experimentation and the use of them to stimulate further experimentation and observation are also found extensively in the writings of scientists and philosophers of science.

From the regularities found in the experiment, conceptual structures are evolved. The value of these conceptual structures depends on its effectiveness to predict further behaviour of nature. These predictions serve as the basis for further experimentation and observation. And so, the scientific edifice appears to be a self renewing, never ending one which continuously builds new conceptual structures through experimentation and analysis of the environment.

The proponents of the 'process approach' in science teaching have attempted to identify the weaknesses of the traditional content-based teaching of science. The defects pointed out by such writers are the following:

i. Over emphasis on information, resulting in a lack of understanding or appreciation of the implications of the content itself.
ii. It makes the learner a passive recipient of second-hand

information with the result that the whole be either unable to create new knowledge or whole fail to appreciate the methods through which new knowledge is created.

iii. Content based teaching and learning is un-psychological and as such implies the wastage of time and effort.

iv. The learner fails to develop real concepts and inter relationships of concepts which are the hallmarks of real scientific understanding (Suresh, 1991).

The supporters of content approach reject the creativity approach because creativity is not believed to be a generalisable and unitary trait that can be trained as such. They also argue that creative functioning in science is not possible with a certain mastery of content.

The proponents of process approach however hold that an initiation into the processes is an essential pre-requisite to a meaningful understanding of content. Creative performances in science are not possible unless specific training is given in that aspect. They argue that a process approach is a good middle ground between content and creativity approaches, drawing content from the scientific disciplines, and using them as illustrative examples to highlight processes. Thus, nurturing the creative use of each process in organising the units of study. This is bound to yield rich dividends in science teaching.

An important outcome of science teaching even under the traditional content based teaching is the ability to apply scientific principles to solve problems. Actually development of problem solving skill is basic to the process approach.

John Dewey's writings, as pointed out earlier, led to the shift in science teaching, based on an understanding of the nature of science and the way science operates. John Dewey's classification of the definition of the steps involved in problem solving, positively led to a highlighting of the immense potentiality of the process approach in science teaching. John Dewey traces the following five steps in the operation of problem solving:

i. The occurrence of a felt difficulty,
ii. definition of the difficulty in terms of problem statement,
iii. Occurrence of a suggested explanation or a problem solution to a given hypothesis, inference or theory,

iv. the rational development of an idea through the development of its implications by means of collecting data, and
v. Correlation of ideas and formulation of concluding belief. These steps have now become the well accepted logical explanation of thought process in science.

An alternative series of steps regarding thinking has been presented by Wallas (1926). The process of thinking, according to Wallas falls into the following four stages: 'preparation, incubation, illumination and verification' (Ebel, 1969). These steps are not in consistent with the steps suggested by Dewey.

Science as Problem Solving

Many modern authorities on science education equate science with problem solving, as an important component of science learning. The UNESCO document (1971) on science education, for example, points out the special nature of processes in science learning by defining science as involving the knowledge of this world and the way of gaining that knowledge. Scientific method according to this document implies asking appropriate questions, seeking relevant answers, setting out the evidence in a clear way and drawing conclusions from this.

Mills and Dean (1960) provide an analysis of the characteristic steps of problem solving through his process oriented inquiry model. The following are the characteristics of the model:

i. Identification of a problem,
ii. Hypothesising a possible solution to the problem,
iii. Gathering data to test the hypothesis,
iv. Revising the hypothesis, and
v. Repeating steps 3 and 4 until the hypothesis which accounts for all the data are found.

A variant of the above is suggested by Smith (1961). The following are the steps in problem solving, according to Smith: Collecting data and interpreting the collected data, reaching conclusions or solutions based only on those particular data and not aside from the data, supplying the conclusions and principles or generalisation to new situations, evaluating the persuasions, discussions, principles ideas and programmes of others.

Taxonomical Approaches in Defining Educational Objectives

One of the most important classifications of educational objectives in terms of human behaviour is available in the taxonomy of educational objectives developed by Bloom (1968) and his associates. This group developed a broad frame work into which all possible behavioural outcomes of education can be fitted, the classification in terms of three major domains viz., the cognitive, affective and psychomotor domains of behaviour. The detailed classifications are now available in Bloom's (1968) classification for cognitive domain, Krathwohl's (1964) works on the affective domain and Simpson's (1966) works on psychomotor domain. Other parallel classifications with in the same framework are also available. Outcomes in science education have also been developed by AAAS (1970)' Nedelsky (1965) and Klopfer (1971).

Bloom's Taxonomy of Educational Objectives

The details of the taxonomical approach by Bloom and his associates are best illustrated by considering the break up of the behavioural objectives in the cognitive domain. The objectives under cognitive domain have been placed in six categories: knowledge, Comprehension, Application, Analysis, Synthesis and Evaluation. The major categories and sub categories of this domain are presented below:

The Cognitive Domain

Knowledge	Knowledge of the specifics	Terminology Specific facts
	Knowledge of ways and means of dealing with specifics	Conventions Trends and sequences Classification and categories Criteria Methodology
	Knowledge of the universals and abstractions in a field	Knowledge of principles and generalisations Knowledge of theories and structures

1. *Knowledge*
   A. Knowledge of the specifics
      - Terminology
      - Specific facts
   B. Knowledge of ways and means of dealing with specifics
      - Conventions
      - Trends and sequences
      - Classification and categories
      - Criteria
      - Methodology
   C. Knowledge of the universals and abstractions in a field
      - Knowledge of principles and generalisations
      - Knowledge of theories and structures
2. *Comprehension*
   A. Translation
   B. Interpretation
   C. Extrapolation
3. *Application*
4. *Analysis*
   A. Analysis of elements
   B. Analysis of relationships
   C. Analysis of organisational principles
5. *Synthesis*
   A. Production of unique communication
   B. Production of a plan or proposed set of operations
   C. Derivatives of a set of abstract relations
5. *Evaluation*
   A. Judgements in terms of internal evidence
   B. Judgements in terms of external criteria

The behaviours from 1 to 6 are arranged in the increasing order of complexity. Equivalent models have been developed for the affective and psychomotor domains as well.

Revised Bloom's Taxonomy

Anderson and Krathwhol (2001) revised Bloom's taxonomy of educational objectives: cognitive domain. The revision serves the purpose of better reflecting what we know about the purpose of teaching, learning and assessment. There are some differences in the revised taxonomy with the original one. The major changes from the original are:

1. The lowest level of the original taxonomy which is labelled as 'knowledge' has been renamed as 'remember'.
2. The two highest level of the original taxonomy have been reversed. i.e. 5th level 'synthesis' and 6th level 'evaluation has been rearranged as 5th level 'evaluation' and 6th level 'create'.
3. Knowledge is redefined as that which is acted on and includes four major dimensions: factual knowledge, conceptual knowledge, procedural knowledge and meta-cognitive knowledge. The first three dimensions in the original taxonomy are retained and the fourth dimension of knowledge is added in the revised taxonomy.

The revised taxonomy also is hierarchical. The levels from lowest to highest are given below.

- Remember: Retrieve relevant information from long term memory; recognise and recall
- Understand : (formerly termed as comprehension) Construct meaning from instructional messages; interpret, exemplify, classify, summarise, infer, compare and explain
- Apply: Use information; execute and implement
- Analyse: Break material into parts and determine the relationship among parts; differentiate, organise and attribute
- Evaluate: Make judgements based on internal and external criteria; check and critique
- Create: Synthesise; put elements together to form new ideas, patterns or structures, generate plan and produce

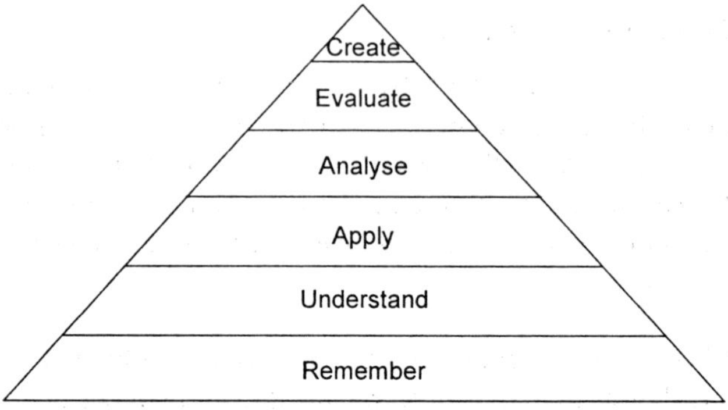

Fig. 4.1: Bloom's Taxonomy-Revised Version

Gagne's Hierarchy of Learning Types

Gagne (1970) has come out with a model based on the hierarchy of learning types. In this model, learning of more basic behaviour is a pre-requisite for learning of the higher order behaviour. The types of learning Gagne classified in order are abbreviated as follows:

1. Signal learning
2. Stimulus response learning
3. Chaining
4. Verbal Association
5. Discrimination learning
6. Concept learning
7. Rule learning
8. Problem solving

Gagne later modified this hierarchy of learning types. He retained the first four in the same order and modified the later four higher types into five varieties of capabilities, as he called them. (Gagne, 1985). These capabilities are:

1. *Intellectual Skills:* Intellectual skills are the most important types of capabilities learned by human beings. It includes, successful handling of symbols for communication with environment. The most typical form of an intellectual skill

is a rule. Intellectual skills consists the following categories:

- Multiple discrimination
- Concrete concept and defined concept
- Higher order principles or learning of rules
- Procedure

II. *Cognitive Strategies:* cognitive strategies are internally organised skills whose functioning is to regulate and monitor the utilisation of concepts and rules. By acquiring and using cognitive strategies, the learners are able to regulate internal processes such as:

- Attending
- Learning
- Remembering
- Thinking
- Problem solving

III. *Verbal Information:* The learner has to learn verbal information and retain it so that, it is immediately accessible. Information is thought of as verbal and capable of being verbalised.

IV. *Motor Skills:* Acquisition of motor skills is the organisation of movements to constitute a total action that is smooth, regular and precisely timed and

V. *Attitude:* Gagne's structure implies the concept of scientific processes as well as those of the complexity of learning skills. Gagne's scheme was used by the American Association for the Advancement of Science and National Foundation for designing a science curriculum.

Nedelsky's Competence: Ability Classification in Science Learning

Nedelsky (1965), has come out with a detailed scheme of classification of competencies or abilities, which may constitute the objectives of a course in one of the physical science in college or high school. They are knowledge, understanding and ability to learn. Each ability is further sub-divided in to those concerned with symbolic (verbal or mathematical) subject matter and those concerned with real phenomena. The abilities under this classification, presented in terms of 'intuitive' and 'laboratory' competencies are given below:

Ability I_1: Knowledge: Verbal and Mathematical
Ability I_2: Understanding: Verbal and Mathematical
Ability I_3: Intuitive Understanding
Ability L_1: Laboratory Understanding
Ability I L2: Intuitive Understanding of phenomena
Ability I_4: Ability to learn
Ability L3: Ability to learn from experiment or observation

(The letters L and I denote 'Laboratory competence and Intuitive understanding respectively).

Table 4.1: Nedelsky's Competence-Ability Classification

Ability I_1	Knowledge: Verbal and Mathematical
Ability I_2	Understanding: Verbal and Mathematical
Ability I_3	Intuitive Understanding
Ability L_1	Laboratory Understanding
Ability I L2	Intuitive Understanding of phenomena
Ability I_4	Ability to learn
Ability L3	Ability to learn from experiment or observation

Classification in Terms of Science Process Skills

A major focus of science instruction over the years has been on the development of reasoning abilities among students. Terms like critical thinking, problem solving, scientific thinking, logical thinking abilities and science process skills have been used to describe the different kinds of reasoning abilities to be developed through science education. Each of these terms has been used to emphasise some unique outcome relating to science, in general the terms reflect some common things. When a student attempts to solve a scientific problem through the manipulation of variables or collection of data, he will be making use of some or all of these abilities (Yeany, *et al.* 1986).

In recent years, two sets of reasoning abilities have taken precedence, each coming from a different theoretical perspective.

These have been labelled 'formal operational reasoning abilities' and the 'integrated science process skills'. Formal reasoning abilities emanate from recent findings of developmental psychology. Abilities under this label include the ability to identify and control variables and to use co-relational, combinational, probabilistic and proportional logic. The integrated science process skills which are expected of science education include abilities which help to identify variables in an experimental situation, ability for hypothesizing, operationally defining, designing experiment and graphing and interpreting data (Yeany, *et al.* 1986).

The AAAS Classification of Science Process Skills

The American Association for the advancement of science (AAAS, 1971) presents thirteen skills (scientific skills) together with a brief definition of each. They are already detailed in chapter II.

Klopfer's Classification of Outcomes in Science

Klopfer (1971) has presented a very exhaustive classification of objectives of science education based on categories of factual knowledge and comprehension, process of scientific inquiry, application of scientific knowledge and methods, manual skills, scientific attitudes and interests and orientation. This is given below in terms of the categories and sub categories.

Table 4.2: Specification for Science Education, Klopfer (1971)

A.0:	**Knowledge and comprehension**	
	A.1:	Knowledge of specific facts
	A.2:	Knowledge of scientific terminology
	A.3:	Knowledge of concepts of science
	A.4:	Knowledge of conventions
	A.5:	Knowledge of trends and sequences
	A.6:	Knowledge of classifications, categories and criteria
	A.7:	Knowledge of scientific technique and procedures
	A.8:	Knowledge of scientific principles and laws
	A.9:	Knowledge of theirs or major conceptual schemes
	A.10:	Identification of knowledge in new contexts
	A.11:	Translation of knowledge from one symbolic form to another

(Contd.)

B.0: Process of scientific inquiry I- Observing and measuring
- B.1: Observation of objects and phenomena
- B.2: Description of observations using appropriate language
- B.3: Measurement of objects and changes
- B.4: Selection of appropriate measuring instruments
- B.5: Estimation of measurements and recognition of limits in accuracy.

C.0: Process of scientific inquiry II - Seeing a problem and seeking ways to solve it
- C.1: Recognition of a problem
- C.2: Formulation of working hypotheses
- C.3: Selection of suitable tests for testing a hypothesis
- C.4: Design of appropriate procedures for performing experiments

D.0: Process of scientific inquiry III- Interpretation of data and formulating Generalisations
- D.1: Processing of experimental data
- D.2: Presentation of data in the form of functional relationship
- D.3: Interpretation of experimental data and observations
- D.4: Extrapolation and interpolation

E.0: Process of scientific inquiry IV- Building, Testing and Revising a theoretical Model
- E.1: Recognition of the need for a theoretical model
- E.2: Formulation of a theoretical model to accommodate knowledge
- E.3: Specification of relationships satisfied by a model
- E.4: Deduction of a new hypothesis from a theoretical model
- E.5: Interpretation and Evaluation of tests of a model
- E.6: Formulation of a revised refined extended model

F.0: Application of scientific knowledge and Methods
- F.1: Application to new problems in the same field of science
- F.2: Application to new problems in a different field of science
- F.3: Application to problems outside of science (including technology)

G.0: Manual skills
- G.1: Development of Skills in using common laboratory equipments

G.2: Performance of common laboratory techniques with care and safety

H.0: Attitudes and interests
- H.1: Manifestation of favourable attitudes towards science and scientists
- H.2: Acceptance of scientific inquiry as a way of thought
- H.3: Adoption of 'scientific attitudes'.
- H.4: Enjoyment in science learning experiences
- H.5: Development of interests in science and science related activities
- H.6: Development of interest in pursuing a career in science

I.0: Orientation
- I.1: Relationship among various types of statements in science
- I.2: Recognition of the philosophical limitations and influence of scientific inquiry
- I.3: Historical perspectives: Recognition of the background of science
- I.4: Realisation of the relationship among science, technology and economics
- I.5: Awareness of the social and moral implications of scientific inquiry and its results.

Process of Science (Nay, Marshal and others)

Nay and others *et al.* (1971) presents the steps in any scientific inquiry as consisting of five major steps viz., initiation, collecting of data, processing of data, conceptualization of data and open-endedness. The scheme places processes in seventeen main sub-divisions and many minor sub-divisions. The scheme excluded so many affective attributes and mental operations such as communication, logical thought, critical attitude, creativity, intention etc. The scheme is presented below:

Initiation

Identifying and formulating a problem

- Speculating about a phenomenon
- Identifying variables
- Noting and making assumptions
- Delimiting the problem

Seeking relevant background information

- Recalling relevant knowledge and experiences
- Doing literature research
- Consulting

Predicting

Hypothesising

Design for collection of data through field work and/or experimentation

- Defining the independent and controlling variables in operational terms
- Defining the procedure and sequencing the steps
- Identifying needed equipment, materials and techniques
- Indicating safety precautions
- Devising the method for recording data

Collection of Data

Procedure

- Collecting, constructing and setting up the apparatus or equipments
- Doing field work and/or performing the experiment
- Identifying the limitation of design (as a result of failures, blind alleys etc., and modifying the procedure (often by trial and error)
- Repeating the experiment (for reproducibility, to overcome the limitations of initiation, design etc.)
- Recording data (describing, tabulating, diagramming, photographing etc.)

Observing and Observations

- Obtaining qualitative data (using senses etc.)
- Obtaining semi qualitative and quantitative data measuring reading scales, calibrating, counting objects or events, estimating, approximating etc.)
- Gathering specimens
- Obtaining graphical data (Charts, photographs, films etc.)
- Noting unexpected or accidental occurrences (serendipity)
- Noting the precision and accuracy of data
- Judging the reliability and validity of data

Processing of Data

Organising the data

- Ordering to identify regularities
- Classifying
- Comparing

Representing the data graphically

- a. Drawing graphs, charts, maps, diagrams etc.
- b. Interpolating, extrapolating etc.

Treating data mathematically

- Computing (calculating)
- Using statistics
- Determining the uncertainty of the results

Conceptualization of Data

Suggesting an explanation

- for a set of data
- deriving an influence or generalisation from a set of data
- Assessing validity of initial assumptions, prediction and hypothesis

Formulating operational definitions

- Verbal
- Mathematical

Expressing data in the Form of Mathematical Relationships

Incorporating the new discovery in to the existing theory (developing a 'Mental model')

Open-endedness

Seeking further evidence to—

- Increase the level of confidence in the explanation or generalization
- Test the range of applicability of the explanation or generalisation

Identifying new problems for investigating because of

- The need to study the effect of new variable
- Anomalous or unexpected observations
- Incompleteness (gaps) and inconsistencies in the theory

Applying the discovered knowledge

Andrew's Classification (1980)

Andrew (1980) classified the abilities of scientific processes into six skills and sixteen sub-skills. They are:

1. Recognising and defining a problem
   - Recognise specific problem in a new situation
   - Isolate the single major idea of problem
   - State problem as definite and concise questions
2. Formulating hypothesis
   - Suggests tentative solutions to the problem
3. Collecting data
   - Select a suitable test for the hypothesis
   - Design experiment
   - Selecting equipment for experiment
   - Observe objects or phenomena
   - Measure objects and changes
4. Interpreting data
   - Organise the collected data
   - Identify relationships
   - Interpret relationships
5. Evaluating hypothesis
   - Formulate conclusions on the basis of relationship found
   - Evaluate hypothesis in relation to data interpreted
6. Formulating Generalizations
   - Apply conclusions to new situations
   - Formulate generalizations on the basis of relationships identified and
   - conclusions formed and applied

UNESCO Approach Relating to Process Outcomes

UNESCO source book for science teaching (1992) lists out the indications of science process skills. They are summarized and given below. Understanding the world around depends on the development of concepts. The development of concepts again depends on process skills. The concepts and process skills are interrelated. As concepts gradually become more sophisticated, process skills need to be refined and extended. In this format investigating is at the centre. The various process skills are emerged from it and again contribute to further investigation.

Observing	• Using the senses (as many as safe and appropriate) to gather information • Identifying differences between similar objects or events • Identifying similarities between different objects or events • Noticing fine details that are relevant to an investigation • Recognising the order in which sequenced events take place • Distinguishing from any observations those which are relevant to the problem at hand
Raising Questions	• Asking questions which lead to inquiry • Asking questions based on hypothesis • Identifying questions which they can answer by their own investigations • Putting questions in to a form, which indicates the investigation which are to are to be carried out • Recognising that some questions cannot be answered by inquiry
Hypothesising	• Attempting to explain observations or relationships in terms of some principle or concept • Applying concepts or knowledge gained in some situation to help understanding or solving a problem in another • Recognising that there can be more than one possible explanation of an event • Recognising the need to test explanation by gathering more evidence • Suggesting explanations which are testable, even if unlikely
Predicting	• Making use of evidence to make a prediction (as opposed to a guess, which takes no account of evidence) • Explicitly use patterns or relationship to make a prediction • Justifying how a prediction was made in terms of present evidence or past experience • Showing caution in making assumptions about the general application of a pattern beyond available evidence • Making use of patterns to extrapolate to cases where no information has been gathered
Finding patterns and relationships	• Putting various pieces of information together from direct observations or secondary sources) and inferring something from them • Finding regularities or trends in information, measurements or observations • Identifying an association between one variable or another

	• Realizing the difference between a conclusion that fits all the evidence and inference that goes beyond it • Checking an inferred association or relationship against evidence
Communicating effectively	• Using writing or speech as a medium for sorting out ideas effectively or linking one idea with another • Listening to others ideas and responding to them • Keeping notes on actions or observations • Displaying results appropriately, using graphs, tables, charts etc. • Reporting events systematically and clearly • Using sources of information • Considering how to present information so that it is understandable by others
Defining and making	• Choosing appropriate materials for constructing things, which have to work or serve a purpose • Choosing appropriate materials for constructing models • Producing plan or design which is a realistic attempt at solving a problem • Succeeding in making models that work or meet certain criteria • Reviewing a plan or a construction in relation to the problem to solved.
Devising and planning investigations	• Deciding what equipment and materials are needed for an investigation • Identifying what is to change or to be changed when different observations or measurements are made • Identifying what variables are to be kept same for a fare test • Identifying what is to be measured or compared • Considering beforehand how the measurements, comparisons etc. are to be used to solve the problem • Deciding the order in which steps to be taken in an investigation
Manipulating materials and equipments effectively	• Handling and manipulating materials with care for safety and efficiency • Using tools effectively and safely • Showing appropriate respect and care for living things • Assembling parts successfully to a plan • Working with the degree of precision appropriate to the task in hand
Measuring and calculating	• Using an appropriate standard or non-standard measure in making comparisons or taking readings • Taking an adequate set of measurements for the task in hand • Using measuring instruments correctly and with reasonable precision • Computing results in an effective way • Showing concern for accuracy in checking

Fig. 4.2: Process Skills as Part of Scientific Investigation
UNESCO Source Book (1992).

Shepardson's Identification of Science Processes

Shepardson (1990) investigated on problem solving phase, student interactions, and thinking skills. He could identify student behaviour behind each phase of the problem solving. They are presented below:

1. *Problem Finding and Refining Phase*: In this phase students employ the following skills:
   a) focussing
   b) analysing
   c) evaluating
   d) integrating
2. *Research Designing Phase*: The students use focussing skills during this phase

3. *Data Collecting Phase*: the skills used by students in this phase are:
    a) focussing
    b) integrating
    c) generating
4. *Data Analyzing Phase*: During this phase the students use the following skills:
    a) remembering
    b) analyzing
    c) organising
    d) information gathering
    e) focussing
    f) integrating
    g) evaluating
5. *Evaluating Phase*: in this phase the skills used are :
    a) organising
    b) focussing
    c) integrating
    d) information gathering

Process Models

Anderson (1970), Wilson, Wilson (1974) and Rachelson (1977) attempt to describe processes in terms of models. Rachelson's (1977) model) model illustrates the relationship between testing and generating a hypothesis. It presents scientific inquiry as a self correcting revisionary system. The revisionary element is critical, as it is the unique characteristics of scientific inquiries (Fig. 4.3).

In Anderson's (1970) model, experimenting is at the apex and observing is at the base. The skills are meaningfully related so that it forms the complete action of inquiry (Fig. 4.4).

Carin and Sund's Model (1970)

Carin and Sund's model (1970) figured (Fig. 4.5) the cyclic nature of new investigations of phenomena in nature, scientific processes and products. As a result of the new investigations of phenomena in nature by using the relevant process skills such as observing, measuring,

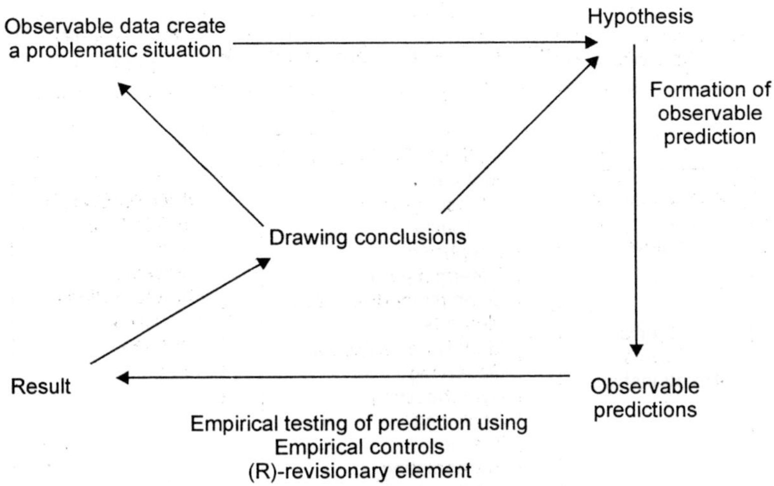

Fig. 4.3: Process of Scientific Inquiry (Rachelson, 1977)

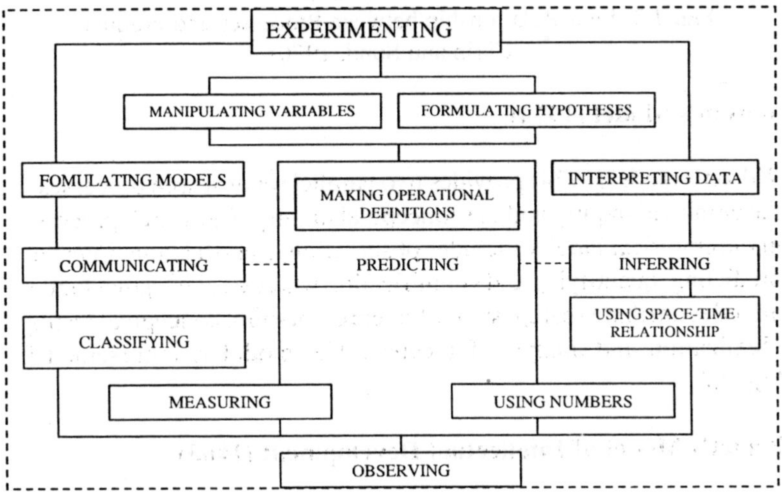

Fig. 4.4: Model of Process Skill (Anderson, 1970)

classifying, analysing, inferring, hypothesising etc., new scientific products are evolved. The products of science again are subjected to observing, synthesising, evaluating etc. will lead to new investigations.

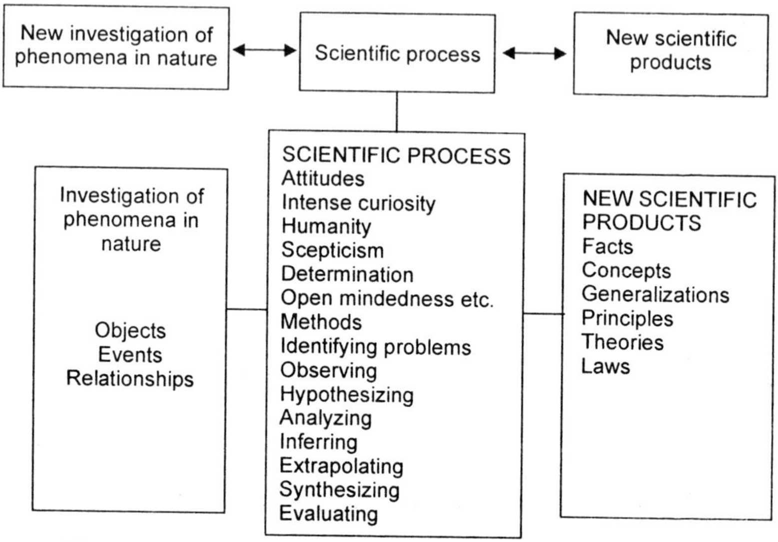

Fig. 4.5: Inter Relationship between Processes and Products (Carin and Sund, 1970)

Wilson's Model (1974)

Wilson's model (1974) provides two parallel set of search processes—the empirical inquiry and the conceptual inquiry. The search processes in the empirical inquiry includes observation, classification, inferring, predicting, quantifying and simplification where as conceptual inquiry includes attribute search, symbolic representation, conceptual testing, idealization and analysis for cause. The model is represented in Fig. 4.6.

Piaget's Model of Intellectual Development (1963)

The typical development of intellectual skills is revealed by Piaget (1963). It starts from the very concrete and specific to the increasingly abstract and general. Highly general intellectual skills are typically formed over a period of stages and ages, and are thought to depend upon the accumulated effects of learning for a considerable variety of relatively concrete principles. Piaget's stages of cognitive development are sensorimotor, preoperational, concrete operational and formal operational.

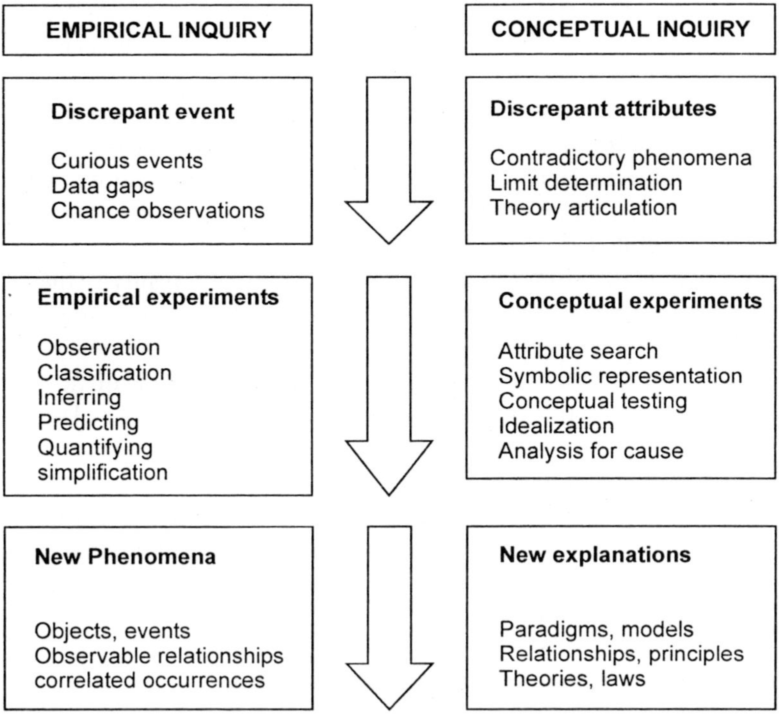

Fig. 4.6: Process Model of Scientific Inquiry (Wilson, 1970)

The Sensorimotor Stage: (from birth to two years of age). During these this stage, infants construct understanding of the world by coordinating their sensory experiences. At the end of this period, the child gets an awareness of object permanence and difference between oneself and surrounding environment.

The Pre-operational Stage: (from two to seven years of age). During this stage the child begins to represent the world with symbol—words and images. This stage has got two substages—symbolic function substage and intuitive thought substage. In symbolic function substage, the ability to represent an object not present develops and symbolic thinking increases. The child exhibits ego-centrism and animism. In intuitive thought substage, the child begins to use primitive reasoning and wants to know the answer to all sorts of questions. The child is sure about his knowledge but he doesn't know how and what he knows. He can concentrate his attention on one characteristic to the exclusion of others. He can admit that some characteristics of an object remain same even though the object might change in appearance.

The Concrete Operational Stage: (from seven to eleven years of age). The child is able for reversible mental action pertaining to real concrete objects. Here logical reasoning in concrete situations starts work. Classification skills are present but ability for abstract thinking lacks. The child can do seriation which is ordering stimuli along with some quantitative dimension. He has the ability of transitivity that is logically combining relations to understand certain conclusions.

The Formal Operational Stage: (from eleven to fourteen years of age). During this stage, thought is more abstract, idealistic and logical. The child thinks like scientists. The child can devise plans to solve problems, and systematically test solutions. He is able to make hypothetico-deductive reasoning.

Piaget's theory was the basis of cognitive constructivism. It figures the nature of cognitive development of an individual. His findings guided many curricular revisions and construction of instructional strategies.

Hierarchical Nature of Science Process Skills

The teaching of science process skills as components of scientific method has always rested on three assumptions:

a) Low level skills can be chained to form higher order skills (Gagne, 1970)
b) Reasoning skills are general, content (domain)-independent skills (Simon, 1981)
c) Thinking skills are independent of the physical and social context in which they are used.

Both information processing psychologists and behaviourists agree that higher order thinking skills can be analyzed into simpler skills and can be learned by synthesizing simpler ones. Cunningham (1984) argues that most of the skills identified by behaviourists and information psychologists are unconnected, arbitrary and non-generative and seem to be a mere collection of isolated tools. Biard and Borich (1987) and Tobin and Capie (1982) conclude that rather than being separate skills, the science process skills are correlated among each other and show high correlations with Piaget's construct of formal reasoning. Roth (1985), on the basis of multilevel hierarchical model and confirmatory factor analysis proposes that all these skills have skills have been shown to be related to one underlying construct. Yap and Yeany (1988) analysed process skill hierarchies in a sample of more than 700 students and found that skills that were presumed subordinate appeared on the top of the hierarchies, and the hierarchies were incompatible for students for students of different reasoning abilities.

It was confirmed from various studies that, expertise depends on a collection of schemata specific to the domain. (Friedler *et al.* 1990, Larkin, 1983). Schon (1983) concluded that content and skills are sophisticatedly interrelated that means become inter dependent with ends, knowing become inseparable from doing. The thinking seems to be domain specific. The efforts to teach general know-how of thinking skills may not succeed. Greeno (1988) suggests that our ability to control and to orchestrate cognitive skills is not an abstract and context free competence which may be easily transferred across other problem areas, but rather consists up on intellectual activities closely tied specifically to the context. The physical and conceptual structure of problems, propose of the activity and social milieu in which it is embedded come under the purview of context. Objects, events, meaning of terms and cognitive activity of an individual become part of the context. As a consequence, performance on the fields of practical problem solving and skill domains advance through the use of situational hints and insight that emerges from tacit knowledge. (Rogolf, 1984; Schon,1987). This ascertains that learning method appropriate to the context is not only meaningful, but also essential. The ideation formulating by such practical situations cannot be replaced by any other types of learning experiences. Herron (1971) argues that such open enquiry, problem oriented teaching learning contexts are essential for science laboratory environments. He found that science laboratory teaching which leaves the problems, the answers, and the method of investigation open for students to be solved was rated highest on a four point "openness of laboratory exercise scale".

Conclusion

In this chapter, we have seen the historical development of science process skills. Its root starts from philosophical thought and reasoning. When reasoning is related to nature, which is the object of science we termed the reasoning process as a scientific inquiry. The required skills for conducting a scientific inquiry or formulating a generalised idea in science are known as science process skills. The skills needed for generating knowledge in other fields of content is known as information processing skills. The skills listed by various authentic sources shows that, though there are some differences in these list all of them possess some general nature. Depending on the context or method, the skills may vary, but a careful coordination of relevant skills will lead to authentic results.

V

Studies on Process Skills

Science process skills are one of the thrust areas for researchers in science teaching. The authors could identify research studies on process skills from 1973 onwards. These studies focussed on different aspects of science process skills. Most of them are experimental in nature conducted in the classroom context. Some are survey studies. An abstract of such studies are detailed below.

Research Studies Focussed Focussing on Science Process Skills

Macbeth (1974) tested the importance of manipulative experience in the attainment of science process skills for kinder garten and third grade students. The study focused on a specific kind of learning task acquisition of science process skills. The investigator taught four kinder garten and four third grade exercises from SAPA programme over a period of fourteen weeks. The data collected from the kinder garten and third grade exercises suggested that the influence of direct first hand manipulative experiences in the development of process skills is more important for the kinder garten children than for older children.

Tomera N. *Audrey (1974)* explored the retention of science processes of observation and comparison in junior high school students. He compared the student abilities to use the science processes of observation and comparison at three intervals—three month, five month and one year period with no formal training, with two week period of training and four weeks period of training. The result showed that the retention ability of comparison and observation and comparison show a high degree of consistency over different time period without any formal raining. As the period increases, the skills also seems to be increased. Regarding the period of training the study reveals that two weeks is was a sufficient period of instruction time. It is was also inferred that once students have been originally instructed, the behaviours inherent in the skills of observation and comparison that they continuously practice them in subsequent learning situations.

Tomera (1974) studied the transfer and retention of transfer of the science processes of observation and comparison in junior high school students. He concludes concluded that the amount of both the processes of observation and comparison which were transferred by the students can be admirably retained over a five month period of no formal training. Again regardless of which set of objects used for training, the students showed ability to transfer the skill to the alternative set of objects, and in turn retain high amounts of the transferred ability.

Anderson et al. (1975) studied the effect of behavioural objectives on immediate learning from an inquiry oriented instructional programme which incorporates knowledge and higher than knowledge level cognitive behaviours as defined by bloom. The treatment was the instruction based on a unit on BSCS Inquiry slides: Structure and function control of blood sugar, a homeostatic mechanism which includes stimuli for knowledge and higher than knowledge level cognitive functioning. The results of this study suggest that under inquiry oriented instructional sequence which are designed to elicit knowledge and higher than knowledge cognitive functioning, the use of behaviourally stated cognitive learning outcomes facilitates immediate learning. An additional conclusion was that facility with scientific process skill enhanced achievement from enquiry oriented biological science materials. The study reinforces reinforced the assumption that objectives enable learners to retain essential points and to organize complex cognitive processes needed for successful inquiry oriented learning experiences.

Cody T. *John and Pizzini l. Edward (1976)* determined the effects of two components of the secondary science teaching programme at the University of Iowa on the development of an understanding of the methods, procedures and processes of science. The two components selected consisted of a research participation programme and a course centered programme. The result revealed that the students in both the research and physics groups showed a gain; significant at the 0.05 level of confidence in their familiarity with the methods and procedures of science as measured by the 'methods and procedures of science test.' On the subtest 'words of science section' the physics group made a significant gain which greatly surpassed the gain of the research participants. The physics group demonstrated a gain significant at the 0.05 level of confidence in their familiarity with the processes of science as measured by the Welsch Science processes Inventory. The research did not show a gain significant at 0.05 level of confidence on the same instrument.

The purpose of the study conducted by *Raven and Calvey (1977)* was to investigate the effects of a process oriented elementary school science programme on the achievement on a test on Piaget's operative comprehension. The results of the study indicate that eighth grade students in the process oriented programme achieved significantly higher scores on operative comprehension items than did eighth grade students in a more traditional programme. They found no differences between the sixth grade groups which could be defined on being in a transitional stage between concrete and formal operations. The process orientation of the experimental group's course programme was a major factor in causing the difference in scores.

Riley P. *Joseph (1979)* compared the effects of hands on versus non-manipulative training in process skills on pre-service teacher's knowledge of process skills understanding of science, and attitude towards science and science teaching and method of instruction. He also investigated the relationship between science grade point average, and the treatment variables. They used 3x3 factorial designs for the study. The two independent variables were science grade point average with three levels designated high, medium and low, and treatment with levels—Active-inquiry treatment level, vicarious-inquiry treatment level and control treatment level. In active inquiry level, the subjects were trained in process skills using, manipulative hands-on approach. Subjects in the vicarious inquiry level group were trained in process skills using the same content of their counterparts, but without student manipulation of science materials. The manipulation of materials was demonstrated by the instructor. Subjects in the control group spent approximately the same amount of time viewing science films dealing with topics such as geology, meteorology and physical science to get a neutral treatment in relation to the two process training approaches. It was concluded from the findings of the study that, training in the science process skills by using vicarious inquiry or active inquiry approach can be employed to improve process skill competence. No treatment effect could be discerned on the dependent variables, attitude towards science and science teaching, understanding science or attitude toward method of instruction. No evidence could be found on any of the criterion measures supporting one inquiry method over the other. Undergraduate grade point average was found to be significantly related to the acquisition of process skills and understanding of science. In general, students had high science grade point averages scored significantly higher on the process and understanding of science instruments than did students having low science point average. The occurrence of interactions on two of the process tests confounds any conclusions about the relationship between science knowledge as measured by science grade point average and science process ability. The nature of the interactions could imply intervention variables not accounted for.

Pappelis, et al. (1980) determined the effectiveness of a semester long course modelled after the AAAS's Science: A Process approach, on the achievement of science process skills. It was found that, using the using the test of science processes as pre and post tests improvement was demonstrated in the thinking skills of medical education preparatory programme students, when SAPA and SAPA like activities used in the curriculum. More specifically significant improvement was made in the skills of measuring, quantifying and inferring. No significant gains were made in observing, experimenting and predicting.

Champagne, et al. (1981) investigated the interaction between semantic knowledge and process and process skills in students' performance involving performance involving two types of problems of problems of inducing structure. The two types of verbal problems are analogies and set membership problems. Both types of problems involved the same science concepts drawn from the discipline of physical geology. The study was carried out in a sectarian urban school, whose students come principally from middle-class homes in the immediate neighbourhood. The sample of the study consists consisted of twenty seven students. It was revealed from the study that, processing skills contribute more to the successful solution of set membership problems than to the solution of analogies problem.

Fraser J. *Barry (1981)* examined the relationship between socio-economic status and proficiency at several inquiry skills important in science education. He used a sample of 1158 seventh grade students in 46 different science classes. He used three separate inquiry skills—using reference, interpreting and processing information and critical thinking in science. It was found that there exists significant relationship for all the three inquiry skills with socio economic status.

Tobin's (1986) study aimed at estimating the relationship between formal reasoning ability, locus of control, academic engagement rates and integrated process skill achievement. The data revealed that attending and generalizing together with formal reasoning are related to achievement Formal reasoning is the strongest predictor of process skill outcomes. The findings underscore the importance of formal reasoning to achievement in science.

The study of *Finely (1982)* determined the extent to which students' knowledge of concepts relevant to mineral classification influence their ability to classify minerals and to find which concepts are most influential. Thirty five eighth grade earth science students were tested regarding their ability to classify minerals correctly (the dependent variable) and their knowledge of minerals, hardness and the logic of classification scheme. (independent variables). The results showed that students' knowledge of relevant concepts substantially influenced their ability to perform the science process of mineral classification.

The purpose of the study of *Padilla, et al. (1983)* was to examine integrated process skill and formal thinking abilities of middle and high school students and determine the relationship, if any, between the two. Resulting correlation shows showed a strong relationship between achievement on the two measures and all subsets of both measures. It could be inferred from the study that process skill teaching might influence formal thinking ability.

Ramesh (1984) found the high ability group following the objective based curriculum achieved higher mean scores than the group following the conventional curriculum. It was also found that the mean scores of the group taught through the objective based curriculum is more effective with respect to the acquisition of process skills than the traditional curriculum group. The above average intelligence group has higher mean scores on the process skill test than average and below average intelligence groups.

Aiello *Nicosia (1984)* investigated the relationship among science teacher characteristics and student outcomes. The selected characteristics of teachers are were their understanding of science processes and their ability to control variables. The student outcomes are were achievement in science content and in processes. The results support the hypothesized relationships and show that the teacher ability to control variables is a more valuable characteristic than the understanding of science processes for student achievement.

The purpose of the study of *Lawrenz and Cohen (1985)* was to examine the attitudes toward science as well as the understanding of the science processes of both elementary and secondary education students prior to taking science methods, immediately after completion of the courses and on completion of their practice teaching experiences. The study also intended to demonstrate how their attitudes and process knowledge differ over time and between levels of preparation. The study indicates indicated that the tendency for both the elementary and secondary education students was toward an increase in knowledge of science processes especially over the practice teaching experience.

Rakow's (1985) study on the influence on student characteristics and classroom characteristics on student's inquiry skill came out with the findings that the model of educational productivity was capable of accounting for between twenty four and thirty two percentage of variance in inquiry skills for the general population of seventeen year olds. He found very little difference in the prediction of inquiry skills for males and females.

Burns, Wise and Okey (1985) reported on the development of test items for assessing identification of variables, statement of hypotheses, operational definitions, design of investigations, and the display and interpretation of data. A pool of items in multiple choice format was developed for these outcomes, examined by experts for content validity, and field tested with students in grades seven through twelve. The resulting test was found to have high reliability and difficulty and discrimination indices with in the range of suggested test development standards.

McKenzie and Padilla (1985) constructed and validated Test of Graphing in Science (TOGS). Skills associated with the construction and interpretations of line graphs were delineated. Nine objectives encompassing these skills were developed. Twenty six items were constructed to measure these objectives. Content validity of the items and objectives was reviewed by a panel of experts who agreed with the test developers on the assignment of test items to objectives. The TOGS was field tested with 119 seventh, ninth and eleventh grade students and revised. It was administered to 387 students in grade seven to twelve. The test proved to be of reasonable validity and reliability.

Lee and Gosby (1985) looked for correlations between the test of science processes and the test of logical thinking. Pre-service elementary teachers grouped as early childhood, intermediate education and college science majors were tested. The investigators found significant differences in the test of science processes between the early childhood education students and college science majors. There was no significant difference between intermediate education group and either of the two groups. The scores on the test of logical thinking, appears to be the best predictor of science process skills. Lee and Gosbi suggested that science teacher educators need to develop science process skills of pre-service teachers. If they wish these people to engage in inquiry teaching and that the science process and logical thinking tests can be used for diagnostic purpose in the pre service programme.

Jones (1985) examined the effects of a science methods course emphasizing mastery over select science process skills on the level of development of logical thinking of pre-service students. 81 juniors enrolled in the methods course were the experimental group. Seniors who had taken a different version of these methods course were the control group. Lawson's group test of logical reasoning was used as pre and post tests. Okey's group test of science processes was also given. Pre-Post comparisons were made using the correlated statistic. Significant differences in growth of logical thinking were found for all levels of cognitive development in the students from the experimental group. Use of the Pearson correlation resulted in the identification of a statistically significant correlation between final logical thinking classification of students and their science process test scores. The use of analysis of variance produced significant differences in favour of the experimental group for post test scores when experimental and control groups were compared.

Yeany et al. (1986) searched for a learning hierarchy among skills comprising formal operations and integrated science processes. Ordering theoretic and probabilistic latent structure methods were used to analyze data on five process skills and six logical thinking skills collected from 700 science students. They identified both linear and branching hierarchical relationships with in and across the two sets of skills. Most of them fit the logical hierarchies which had guided curriculum development and classroom practices in the past. But a few—identifying variables super ordinate to control of variables—run counter to our present logic and understanding of these skills. Conservation reasoning, combinational reasoning and design experiments form the base of the hierarchy. Students who have mastered these skills are more probable to the ones who develop the next level skills. At the next level they found the skills of graphing and interpreting data, operationally defining, controlling variables, and proportional reasoning. These skills appear to be subordinate to the three skills—conservation reasoning, Combinational reasoning and design experiments—and sub ordinate to the other four skills—identifying hypotheses, probability reasoning, identifying variables and co-relational reasoning. They recommended that the entry level, as well as progress of students in relation to the skills must also be measured regularly to determine the status of the individual and to prescribe instruction responsive to task related prerequisite skills lacking in the student. Further, they suggest that researchers should use the measurement and statistical procedures that exist to establish the hierarchical relationships among the set of concepts and skills identified as those to be obtained by a scientifically literate individual.

In an extension of this study *Yeany and Yap (1988)* explored the possible hierarchical relationships among Piagetian cognitive modes and integrated science process skills for the concrete, transitional and formal reasoning levels. Among the possible hierarchical relationships they identified the best suitable hierarchical relationship for each reasoning levels and observed positive vertical transfers.

Adey and Harien (1986) analyzed test items used to survey the attainment of science process skills in a representative sample of eleven year olds in Britain to determine the level of demand, in Piagetian terms, made by each item. It was found that the level of cognitive demand was a reliable predictor of the limiting difficulty of an item. The difference between potential difficulty as measured by supposed demand level and the actual difficulty encountered by subjects revealed areas in the curriculum where further effort in teacher education and curriculum development would be profitable. The study provided some evidence for an inherent hierarchy of process skills.

Tobin (1986) studied the student tasks involvement and achievement in process oriented science activities using a sample of students from fifteen intact classes in grades six and seven from suburban schools in Perth, Australia. The results of the study indicated that student's reasoning ability and engagement in planning and collecting tasks are positively related to achievement. It is possible that concrete data collecting activities facilitate an understanding of planning and data processing skills that reflected in higher achievement scores. The study also reaffirms reaffirmed the relationship between formal reasoning ability and process skill achievement. Significant relationships were also obtained for student achievement and engagement in planning and collecting tasks.

Khalwania (1986) developed a concept based curriculum and tested its efficiency in developing cognitive structures and acquisition of process skills. The study involved four independent factors, namely curriculum types, self concept, intelligence and socio economic status. There were two criterion variables namely process skills and cognitive structures. The study revealed that (1) High socio economic status group did equally well in the acquisition of process skills in science, (2) The low socio economic group following the concept based curriculum scored significantly higher on process skills than the high self concept and high SES groups using the conventional curriculum. When low ability student having low SES, taught the concept based curriculum scored higher on the process skill test than students having high self concept and low SES but taught through conventional curriculum.

The study conducted by *Paulose (1987)* or on process outcomes in learning of Physics of university entrants; the role of manifest anxiety in combination with sex and residence of subjects, revealed that those with manifest anxiety will, remaining the other factors (sex, residence) remaining same, achieved higher in science when achievement is was conceived in terms of process outcomes in physics.

Strawitz and Malone (1987) compared the effects of two methods of instruction designed to teach pre-service elementary teachers to acquire and retain integrated science process skills. In one section, instruction was provided by the teacher, where as in the other section, instruction was provided by using written self instructional materials. Results indicate that the self instructional method is significantly more effective than the teacher directed method. It was found that both treatments produce long lasting retention effects.

Tamir and Amir (1988) analysed inquiry oriented practical matriculation tests of 3650 12th grade biology students in Israel to find out the inter relationships among twenty one process skills. Using correlation and vari max factor analysis, seven factors were obtained. These factors are—

1. Handling quantitative relationships
2. Explaining and assessing data
3. Conceptualising and planning investigations
4. Summarizing results
5. Interpreting and concluding
6. Selecting forms for presenting findings
7. Designing experiments.

Exploration of the effect of directed inquiry approach, integrating several learning strategies such as advance organizers, the learning cycle, concept maps, etc, on learning of science process skills by *Germann (1989)* reports reported that the directed inquiry approach to learning has had no significant effect on the learning of science process skills or on cognitive development.

Varghese (1989) studied the affective correlates of process outcomes in biology by using a sample of 800 secondary school students. The study came out with the results that a statistically significant positive relationship exists between process outcomes in biology with attitude towards problem solving, mathematics, science and science interest.

Lobo (1990) explored the effect of developing Science Process Outcomes among pre-service secondary school science teachers on their classroom behaviour. It was observed from the study that as a result of Process Outcomes, student teachers tend to be more heuristic, problem solving oriented and speculative in contrast with those who are not given this training.

Suresh (1991) conducted a study on Identification of certain Sociological, Cognitive, and Environmental variables related to Process Outcomes in secondary school Biology and found that parental education, Parental Occupation, Parental Income, family Size and Socio-economic status coming under the Sociological variables and Intelligence and Science learning approach coming under the cognitive variables and Home environment for science learning and total science learning environment and science learning environment—student initiated are significantly influencing process outcomes in Biology. A multiple prediction equation was also developed for predicting process outcomes using the four best predictors among the independent variables, viz.; intelligence, parental education, parental occupation and science learning approach

Piura Michel and Baker R. Dale (1991) designed and evaluated a high school curriculum to teach scientific literacy. They examined the effect of the curriculum on process skills, cognitive ability and attitude of students in the first year of high school. They examined whether it was possible to teach scientific skills and whether a literacy curriculum affects attitude and cognitive ability. Two hundred and fifty ninth standard students were enrolled in a specially designed literacy course which met for three hours and twenty minutes each week for thirty nine weeks. Students were pre-tested for mathematical, spatial logical and verbal abilities as well as for attitude towards self and science and psychological type. The course was successful in the teaching of skills. In addition, there was significant increase in spatial, verbal and quantitative abilities.

Singh and Black (1991) conducted a study to find out the effect of task contexts on pupils' performance in science process skills. The study revealed that there exist an apparent interaction between process skills and contexts. Pupil's achievement on the interpretation skills significantly was higher in everyday contexts than in scientific contexts. For application skills, it was significantly higher in scientific contexts.

Ampili (1991) in her study assessed separately the possible relationship of process outcomes in science to science interest, scientific attitude towards academic work of total sample and relevant sub-samples. She found a positive and significant relationship between process outcomes and science interest, scientific attitude and attitude towards academic work.

Using a sample of 64 Ninth grade high school biology students, *Edison (1992)* examined the relationship of microcomputer graphics and alpha numeric models of data presentation with students' process skills and conceptual understanding of selected genetics concepts. This study reveals that the microcomputer graphics and alphanumeric models of data presentation resulted in students' ability to use specific process skills in problem solving.

Matteheis, et al. (1992) assessed the status of certain reasoning and process skills in junior and high school students and to make comparison between students in North Karolina and Japan. The study examined the relationship between developmental levels of thinking and integrated process skills. The results showed that Japanese students in grades 7, 8 and 9 performed significantly better in measuring, logical reasoning and integrated process skills than North Karolina students. It was also showed that Japanese and north Karolina students improve in reasoning and process skills as they progress from seventh to ninth grades. A moderately strong and almost identical correlation was found to exist between the reasoning skills as measured by the Group Assessment of logical thinking test, and integrated process skills as measured by the test of integrated process skills.

The study conducted by *Roth, et al. (1993)* examined the development of integrated science process skills in the context of open-inquiry laboratory sections. The approach of study was post qualitative. The results showed that students developed higher order process skills through non-traditional laboratory experiences that provided the students with freedom for experiments of personal relevance in authentic contexts. Students learned to

a) Identify and define pertinent variables
b) Interpret transform and analyze data
c) Plan and design an experiment
d) Formulate hypotheses

The study suggests that process skills need not be taught separately. Integrated process skills develop gradually and reach a high level of sophistication when experiments are performed in meaningful contexts.

The study conducted by *Paulose (1987)* or process outcomes in learning of Physics of university entrants; the role of manifest anxiety in combination with sex and residence of subjects, reveals that those with manifest anxiety will, the other factors (sex, residence) remaining same, achieve higher in science when achievement is conceived in terms of process outcomes in physics.

Hamil (1994) investigated the process skill proficiency and problem solving perceptions of pre-service elementary science teachers enrolled in fundamentals of science teaching. The findings of the study support the following recommendations for pre-service teacher education programmes, (1) process skill instruction should be included in the instructional programmes through the use of a process skill unit in content area or in a process skill methods course, and (2) educators should consider the possibility that formal reasoning ability and process skill proficiency may be distinguishable competencies.

Kok-Aunton (1994) examined the generalizability of Science Process Outcomes for students carrying out whole investigations, using a sample of 135 eighth graders in Singapore. The study showed that the skills of preliminary trials, planning, communicating and interpreting are generalisable.

Germann and Aram (1996) assessed the students' performance on the science processes of recording data, analyzing data, drawing conclusions, and providing evidence. A total of 304 students were field tested by the alternative assessment of science process skills. Their responses were used to develop a research rubric, and then this rubric was used to determine response patterns that could inform both instruction and assessment of science process skills. Only 61 per cent of students performed the activity and recorded data successfully. 69 per cent of students did not attend to the hypotheses in drawing conclusions. 81 per cent did not provide specific evidence for their conclusions.

Celene (1998) conducted a study of Process Outcomes in Physics in relation to some select cognitive, affective, social and environmental variables'. The study revealed that all the cognitive, affective and social variables correlate significantly with process outcomes in physics. The multiple correlation coefficients 'R' between process outcomes in physics and the four highly correlated independent variables indicated that the independent variables acting together exert a significant influence on 'Process Outcomes in Physics'.

Jyothis (1999) conducted "A study on the factors affecting problem solving skills in physics of ninth standard students of Kannur district". The study revealed that the mean of scores of boys were significantly higher than that of girls and there was significant difference between the problem solving skills in physics viz., observation, classification, formulating hypothesis, testing hypothesis, analysis and inference, of standard nine students of aided and government schools in Kannur district.

Antu (2000) in her study on process outcomes in basic science of primary school children found no significant correlation between personal adjustment and process outcomes of boys, rural school children and private school children. Mean scores of process outcomes of students in sub samples classified on the basis of (a) sex (b) school location and (c) type of school management differed significantly.

Walters, et al. (2001) determined Jamaican high school students' level of performance on five integrated process skills and if there were statistically significant differences in their performance linked to their gender, grade level, school location, school type, student type and socio-economic background. The result indicated that the subjects mean score was low and unsatisfactory; (2) their performance in decreasing order was interpreting data, recording data, generalizing formulating hypotheses and identifying variables; (3) There were statistically significant differences in their performance based on their grade level, school type, student type, and socio-economic background. There was a positive, statistically significant and fairly strong relationship between their performance and school type, but weak relationships among student type, grade level and socio-economic background S and performance.

Huppert, et al. (2002) investigated the computer simulations impact on students' academic achievement and on their mastery of science process skills in relation to their cognitive stages. The results indicate that the concrete and transition operational students in the experimental group achieved significantly higher academic achievement than their counterparts in the control group. The higher the cognitive operational stage, the higher students' achievement was, except in the control group where students in the concrete and transition operational stages did not differ. Goals achieved equally with the boys in the experimental group.

Saat (2004) examined the process of acquisition of integrated science process skills, particularly the skill of controlling variables, in a web-based learning environment among grade 5 children. Data were gathered primarily from children's conversations and teacher-student conversations. Analysis of the data revealed that the children acquired the skills in three phases from the phase of recognition to the phase of familiarization and finally to the phase of automation. Nevertheless, the acquisition of the skill only involved the acquisition of certain sub skills of the skill of controlling variables.

Jones, (2005) et al. explored children's theory—prediction consistency in a computer mediated task in which multiple opportunities were provided to predict outcomes and review theories. An initial correlation study revealed that theory-prediction consistency was associated with children's success when attempting to identify causation. The second study investigated the effect of goal and a simple intervention upon children's theory—prediction consistency. It was found that the type of goal has no effect, but the intervention which encouraged the children to use their theory to make prediction, significantly improved their ability to identify cause.

Celene (2006) compared the provision offered by ICT integrated approach and constructivist approach for student engagement in science processes. Analysis of processes revealed that value of actual experiments provides rich experience. Provision for science processes are involved more in constructivist approach where learning is constructed on the basis of real live experiences.

Geevarughese, (2007) made conducted a study on school related variables and Process Outcomes in mathematics at the secondary school stage. One of the major findings of the study was that process outcomes are highly correlated to learning environment. Another finding of the study was that the process outcomes are very much related to teacher effectiveness.

Umadevi, M.R. (2008) made designed an experimental study for enhancing the process outcomes in biology through biological science inquiry Model. The result of the study revealed that the biological science inquiry model has been found to be more effective than the conventional method in teaching biology.

Devanathan, (2010) focused on a study on the efficacy of project based learning strategies on process outcomes in biological science in correlation with science interest. The study showed that project based learning group students were attaining significantly higher scores than the students taught through conventional method

Conclusion

A thorough observation of these studies gives a vivid picture of research on process outcomes, the effort to develop process outcomes in relation to school subjects and its correlates. Some studies revealed the need of adopting special instructional strategies for developing science process skills such as providing manipulative experience. Some compared the relationship between different components. Some studies explored the transfer and retention of science process skills and its various components. Findings suggested that intelligence, attitude towards science learning, interest in science learning, socio-economic status 'preparation for examination, reading and note taking, school environment, habits of concentration etc., are capable of predicting the process outcomes in school subjects. The findings of these studies show a positive relationship exist between process outcomes in various school subjects with the variables broadly falling under cognitive, affective, social and environmental parameters.

VI

Teaching of Science Process Skills

It is a matter of debate among science educators that science process skills are acquired through science education as a by-product or as a result of special training. Some research studies show that, specially designed instructional programmes are effective in developing science process skills at different levels. Apart from the adoption of specially designed instructional programmes, science teaching in classroom should be capable of inculcating science process skills among students. In order to meet these goals, interesting hands on experiments and activities should be included in the teaching learning process which stimulate students quest for inquiry. Science classes should be busy with observation, arranging apparatus and materials, measuring, organising data, drawing inference, hypothesising, designing simple experiments, testing hypothesis, and drawing generalisations. Those activities which include, as much as process skills should be there in each lesson according to the nature of the topic.

Strategies and Sample Lesson Plans for Developing Science Process Skills

Some model lesson plans, which will help for developing science process skills among students, are given below. Each lesson plan follows different approaches and instructional strategies, but all of them share a common ground; they provide a platform for developing science process skills among students. These lesson plans are based on constructivist approach, information processing models of teaching such as concept attainment model and inquiry training model, cognitive apprenticeship model, conceptual change model such as 7E learning cycle, goal based scenario model and problem based learning. For each of these lessons, the focus is on different aspects of science process skills, but the impact of them is valuable.

Constructivist Teaching Strategy

Constructivist approach was viewed as a theory of learning, rather than a prescription for teaching methods in its beginning. But now, it is considered as an active reform, and has started experimentally and reported the instructional practices which help teachers nurture students' independent thinking and knowledge construction. Constructivism is based on the belief that learners actively create, interpret and organize knowledge in their own ways. These intellectual transformations occur when individual reconsider new instructional experiences with existing cultural and social knowledge and contexts in which the ideas occur.

The instructional strategies based on constructivist approach suggest that students should participate in experiences that accommodate inquiry activities, discovery, problem solving, discussion with peers and teachers, collecting and interpreting information from different sources, expressing their understanding in diverse ways and applying and validating their understanding in new ways. In order to meet these goals, the teachers must provide alternating learning situations, complex learning environment and opportunities for negotiations.

LESSON PLAN
BASED ON CONSTRUCTIVIST APPROACH

Subject: Physics | *Standard*: VIII
Unit: Motion | *Topic*: Speed
Duration: 40'

Content Overview

The content of the teaching manual includes the concepts of distance and speed.

Content Analysis

Terms

1. Distance
2. Speed

Facts

1. Every body in the universe undergoes motion.
2. Speed is expressed in terms of distance and time.

Concepts

- Distance: Length travelled by an object
- Speed: The distance travelled by an object in unit time
- *Units:*
- The unit of distance is meter.
- The unit of speed is m/s
- The unit of time is second.

Definitions

- The length travelled by an object is distance.
- Speed is the distance travelled by an object in unit time.

Science Process Skills

The following science process skills will be emphasized during the execution of lessons.

- Observes distance and speed
- Measures distance and speed
- Organize data meaningfully
- Defines operationally distance and speed
- Explains speed
- Conducts experiment to measure speed
- Draws inference about the relationship between distance and speed
- Generalizing ideas regarding speed

Curricular Objectives

Through discussion and group activities, the pupil develops:

- the knowledge and understanding about speed.

- the science process skills required to generate the knowledge regarding distance and speed.
- the science process skills to apply the knowledge in familiar and unfamiliar situations.

Domain of objectives	Specific objective
Knowledge	recalls distance
	recognizes distance
	recognizes speed
	defines speed
Process	explains speed
	conducts experiment to measure speed
	establishes the relationship between distance and speed
Application	synthesizes different ideas regarding speed
	consolidates ideas on distance and speed
	applies the knowledge to new and familiar situations
Creativity	gives multiple responses to questions on speed.
Attitude	sees the relationship between distance and speed
	being curious to know more about speed
	shows spirit of team work, self help and self reliance
	develops the sense of dedication

Teaching-Learning Strategies

i. Group activity
ii. Demonstration
iii. Discussion

Pre-conceptions/Pre-requisites

Students should have the knowledge about motion, distance and time.

Resources and Support Materials

6 stop watches, charts showing the definition of speed.

Process/Activity **Evaluation**

Sensitisation

Teacher: Lack of knowledge about speed causes lack of awareness about the universe and our surroundings. We are part of this universe. When we look around our surroundings, we see all objects are moving. Motion of leaves, motion of hands and legs, motion of birds etc., are some among them. But many of the motions in our surroundings are not observable or tangible. All the motions have different properties. Whether the time taken to reach school is the same when you are travelling by bus or when you walk to school? Today we will learn some details of motion of which we are also forming a part.
By listening to the introduction given by teacher, students become interested to learn the details of motion.
At this stage, students are divided in to different groups for class room activities.

No. of groups: 6
No. of activities: 3

Timing

Introduction: 5'
Activity 1: 10'
Activity 2: 10'
Activity 3: 10'
Conclusion: 5'.

Group Discussion

A picture of 'back of the travelling bus in which speed limit in cities is written as '35 kmph' is given to all the groups. Students observe the picture and the meaning of the communication '35 kmph' and write their inference in their science notebook.

Tips for Discussion

- 'kmph' refers to what?
- Why speed limit '35 kmph' is written in the back of the buses?

Each group presents their findings in the whole group. The teacher consolidates students' ideas and gives the standard scientific information if necessary.

Group Activity II

Students are going to the school ground for group activity. One student from each group runs for a distance of 100ms. The others observe the race and record the time taken by them by using stop watch.

Students answer the questions given below:

- How much the distance they run?
- How much time is taken to cover this distance?
- How much distance they run within one second?

By answering these questions students define speed as the distance travelled by an object in unit time. Students formulate the formula for speed as Distance travelled/Time

Consolidation

Speed is the distance travelled by an object in unit time. Unit time may be 1 second, 1 minute or one hour.

Speed = Distance travelled/time

Group Activity III

Students are given a work sheet to fill as a result of group work.

- A car travels a distance of 120 kms in two hours and a bus travels a distance of 150 kms in three hours. Then,
- Calculate the distance travelled by each vehicle in one hour.
- Which of the vehicles has greater speed?
- Find out the speed of a cycle which travels 50ms in 10 seconds.
- What inference you can draw regarding the unit of speed from these two cases?

Consolidation

The unit of speed may be kilometre/hour, kilometer/sec, meter/sec, meter/hour etc.

Group Activity IV

Students find out the meaning of writing '35 kmph' written at the back of the travelling buses. Speed limit 35 kmph means the speed of the bus should not exceed 35 kilometer in one hour in cities.

Application

- Awareness about speed limit helps students to become acquainted with traffic rules and avoid accidents.
- Distance travelled by an object can be calculated if speed and time are given.

Follow-up Activities

- Define speed. How can it be calculated?
- Write a report on recent motor accidents and their reasons.

COGNITIVE APPRENTICESHIP MODEL

Cognitive Apprenticeship refers to the focus on learning through guided experience in cognitive skills and processes, rather than physical ones. Although we do not wish to draw a major theoretical distinction between the learning of physical and cognitive skills, there are differences that have practical implications for the organization of teaching and learning activities (Collins, 1991). Cognitive Apprenticeships are situated within the social constructivist paradigm. They suggest students work in teams on projects or problems with close scaffolding of the instructor. Cognitive Apprenticeships are representative of Vygotskian "Zone of proximal development"; in which student tasks are slightly more difficult than students can manage independently, requiring the said of their peers and instructor to succeed.

Cognitive Apprenticeship works off of the theory of the Zone of Proximal Development (ZPD), that refers to the Zone of development that is located in between what a student can successfully do on his/her own and what the learner will be able to do in the future. With the guidance of an adult the student may be able to move on to the next stage of learning. Through interaction the model allows the student to be successful at a skill or task that may be too complex for them to handle and expands his/her cognitive abilities.

Teaching Strategies in Cognitive Apprenticeship

A Cognitive Apprenticeship environment allows both teachers and students to demonstrate and share their expertise. In this setting, the teacher's goal is to help students gradually take on more complex forms of reasoning and performance through observation and guided practice. Allan Collins and his colleagues describe three core teaching methods in a Cognitive Apprenticeship—Modelling, Coaching and Scaffolding—designed to support students' emerging skills.

Modelling

The apprentice observes the expert demonstrate the different parts of the task. The expert makes the various components of the task visible to the novice. The issue of observation is critical here. The expert provides the conduct of the activity but also provides the learner with a task overview that serves as an advanced organizer for future observation sessions with the expert or with others (expert or not) where much of the learning occurs.

Scaffolding

The support provided by the expert as the novice attempts the task. This support is in the form needed by the novice in the conduct of the task and is sensitive to the issues of novice learning. There may be differing types of scaffolding, i.e., scaffolding that is dependent on the task type. In a team setting such difference need the appropriate consideration. When a teacher provides scaffolding, the teacher executes parts of the task that the student cannot yet manage.

Coaching

Coaching consists of observing students while they carry out a task and offering hints, scaffolding, feedback, modelling, reminders, and new tasks aimed at bringing their performance closer to expert performance. Coaching may direct students' attention to a previously un-noticed aspect of the task or simply remind them of some aspect of the task that is known but has been temporarily overlooked. The content of the coaching interaction is immediately related to specific events or problems that arise as the students' attempt to accomplish the target task (Collins, Brown, and Newman, 1989).

LESSON PLAN
BASED ON COGNITIVE APPRENTICESHIP MODEL

Name of the teacher: Sonia Kurian *Subject*: Physics
Unit: Fluids *Std.*: IX
Topic: Surface Tension *Time*: 40 minutes

Content Overview

Surface Tension: The force reducing the surface area of a liquid surface or liquid membrane is called surface tension.

Content Analysis

Terms

Surface Tension

Facts

- The direction of the resultant force on the liquid surface is in downward direction.
- The resultant force acting on the molecules inside a liquid is zero.
- The liquid surface can act like a stretched membrane.
- Surface force tries to reduce the surface area.

Concept

Surface Tension: The force which causes the liquid surface to act like a stretched membrane.

Definition

Surface Tension: The force reducing the surface area of a liquid surface or liquid membrane is called surface tension.

Curricular Objectives

- The pupil develops knowledge and understanding of the scientific terms, facts, concepts etc regarding surface tension.
- The pupil acquires skills for generating the concepts and apply them in familiar and unfamiliar situations

Specific Objectives

The pupil

- recalls adhesion and cohesion
- asks questions about surface tension
- defines operationally surface tension
- conducts experiment
- asks questions which lead to inquiry
- identifies questions, which the student can answer by his/her own investigation
- develops lateral thinking related to surface tension
- adopts scientific and systematic procedures of work
- observes and recognizes physical surroundings both natural and manmade
- develops simple experiments to show surface tension.

Instructional Strategies

The teacher adopts Cognitive Apprenticeship Model.

Pre-Requisites

The pupil should have knowledge about adhesion and cohesion.

Learning Materials

- Ordinary classroom equipments.
- Charts: shows the definition of surface tension.
- Materials like beaker, soap water, needle, and tissue paper.

Teacher Activity	Pupil Activity
Modelling	
A clean needle is placed on a piece of tissue paper or on a newspaper. Carefully place the paper on the surface of the water taken in a beaker and wait patiently. Teacher asks the pupil to observe what happened.	Pupils observe the experiment and find tissue paper becomes wet and the needle floats on the surface of water and they record their observations.
The teacher asks the pupils what happened when a razor blade is placed gently on the surface of the water.	Pupils get the idea about surface tension.

(Contd.)

Teacher Activity	Pupil Activity
The force which causes the liquid surface to act like a stretched membrane is called surface tension.	Pupils can understand clearly the idea about surface tension through the chart.
Teacher clears the pupils' doubts.	Pupils ask some questions to the teacher related to the topic.
Scaffolding	
Prepare a concentrated soap solution in a beaker. Dip a metal wire loop in it. It can be seen that a soap film is formed on it. Form a closed loop with a thin cotton thread. The cotton thread is made wet with soap solution and placed on the soap film carefully. Break the soap film within the cotton loop with a needle. The teacher suggests the pupils to observe and write the result. Teacher evaluates the discussion written on flash cards.	On observation, pupils could see that the soap film acts like a stretched membrane and the soap film tries to reduce the area. In this experiment, force is acting on the surface of the liquid and this force is the surface force and this is marked. Pupils mark the results on flash cards on the basis of their group discussion.
The resultant force experienced on a molecule on the liquid surface is not zero. It acts downwards. As a result of it, the liquid surface will act as a stretched membrane. This has a tendency to reduce the surface area. Thus the molecules at the surface attract each other with a force. This is the reason for the surface tension.	Pupils mark the results on the flash card on the basis of their group discussions.
Teacher clears the pupils' doubts.	Pupils ask some questions to the teacher related to this topic.
Coaching	
Teacher asks the pupils to find why the liquid drops are spherical in shape.	Spherical shape has least surface area compared to all other shapes. The liquid surface has a tendency to keep least surface tension. Surface

(*Contd.*)

Teacher Activity	Pupil Activity
	tension is least when the surface area is minimum. The rain drops are spherical in shape because it has a tendency to keep least surface area n order to have a low surface tension. Pupils understand this and record their understanding.
Teacher motivates the pupil to suggest possible reasons for hot water is more effective than cold water in cleaning dirt.	Pupil suggests that hot water has less surface tension than cold water.
Teacher clears the pupils' doubts.	Pupils ask some doubts to the teacher related to this topic.

Review

Student show that on the basis of group discussion and experiments, we understand the surface tension and we found some instances in our daily life related to surface tension.

What is surface tension?

Assignment

Why do motor mechanics use kerosene for cleaning oily hands?

Lesson Plan 2
Based on Cognitive Apprenticeship Model

Name of the teacher: Sonia Kurian
Name of the School: H.S.S. Karimba
Std.: IX
Strength: 31

Subject: Physics
Unit: Fluids
Topic: Pressure and Thrust
Time: 40 minutes

Content Overview

This portion includes pressure and thrust.

Thrust: The total force acting normal to a surface is thrust.

Pressure: The force acting normal to a unit area is pressure.

Content Analysis

Terms

Pressure, Thrust

Facts

- Pressure increases with decrease in surface area.
- Pressure decreases with increase in surface area.

Concept

Pressure, Thrust

Definition

Thrust: The total force acting normal to a surface is called thrust.
Pressure: The normal force acting per unit area is called pressure.

Curricular Objectives

The pupil develops knowledge and understanding of the scientific terms, facts, concepts etc regarding Pressure and Thrust.

Specific Objectives

The pupil

- recalls the term pressure.
- develops relevant process skills to generate the above mentioned concepts, facts etc.
- asks questions about pressure and thrust.
- defines operationally Pressure and Thrust.
- applies the knowledge and process skills related to Pressure and Thrust.
- The pupil
- observes the experiment.
- asks questions which lead to inquiry.
- identifies questions, which he/she can answer by his/her own investigation.
- develops lateral thinking related to pressure and thrust.
- adopts scientific and systematic procedures of work.
- observes and recognizes physical surroundings both natural and manmade.
- develops simple experiments to show Pressure and Thrust.

Instructional Strategies

The teacher adopts Cognitive Apprenticeship Model.

Pre-Requisites

The pupil should have knowledge about Pressure and Area.

Learning Materials

Ordinary classroom equipments

Charts: showing the definition of Pressure and Thrust.

Teacher Activity	Pupil Activity
Modelling	
Teacher suggests the pupils to write down some features which are common to liquids and gases. Liquids and gases having these common features are together known as fluids.	They have no definite shape. They have more freedom in movement. Liquids can flow easily. These features are written down on the basis of pupil's observations.
Take and find the weight of a brick. Then place the brick with its broad side on a table and its boundaries are marked. Teacher suggests the pupils to find how much force is exerted by the brick on the table. How much is the area on which this force is exerted?	Pupil writes down the details in the table on the basis of doing the experiment.
Find out the area of contact of the brick when it is placed. Is there any change in the force exerted in the different cases? Write down the details which you have got in the table.	
The total force acting normal to a surface is known as Thrust. The normal force acting per unit area is called pressure. Pressure P = F / A The unit of pressure is Pascal. $1 \text{ Pa} = 1\frac{\text{N}}{\text{m}^3}$	On seeing the chart, pupils can understand the idea about Thrust and Pressure.
Teacher clears pupils' doubts.	Pupils ask some doubts to the teacher related to this topic.

(Contd.)

Teacher Activity	Pupil Activity
Scaffolding	
Take a wide tray and spread a thick layer of sand on it. Remove the lid of a tiffin box and place the box on the sand with its open side up. Place a heavy object in the box. Now empty the box. The box is placed upside down on the sand and the same object placed upon it. Teacher suggests to mark what difference you do observe. Pressure increases with decrease in surface area. It is difficult to cut a tree with a blunt axe. Teacher suggests to find the explanation for this on the basis of group discussion.	On the basis of the experiment they find and write down what happens when box is placed upside down on the sand and the object is placed upon it. As a result of group discussion, they find and mark pressure increases with decrease in surface area.
Teacher clears the pupils' doubt.	Pupils ask some questions to the teacher related to this topic.
Coaching	
Using a wooden plank you can walk over slushy mud without sinking into it. Teacher demands to pupil to find the reason for this.	Pupils found and write down the principle. The pressure decreases with increase in surface area.
A sharp nail pierces more easily through wood than a blunt nail. Teacher suggest to pupil to find the reason for this one.	Pupils found and write down the principle. The pressure increases with decrease in surface area.
Teacher clears the pupils' doubts.	Pupils ask some doubt to the teacher about this topic.

Review

On the basis of group discussion and doing experiments pupils understand the idea about pressure and thrust and also find some closely related instances n our daily life related to this topic.

Ducks can walk easily over mud. Why?

Assignment

The area of the top surface of a table with four legs is $2m^2$ and the cross sectional area of each leg is $0.0025\ m^2$. If the weight of the table is 500N, find out the pressure in each case given below.

(i) When the table is placed with its top touching the ground?

(ii) When it is placed on its legs?

CONCEPT ATTAINMENT MODEL

Concept attainment model of teaching has been presented by Bruner, Goodnow and Austin. This model has been developed from the study of thinking. This model is concerned with two separate but related ideas: the nature of concepts themselves and the thinking processes used by individuals to learn concepts. Bruner's ideas regarding this have been shaped into a model of teaching by Bruce Joyce and Marsha Weil (1980).

Nature of Concepts

A concept is an ideation or a mental picture of objects, events, symbols or experience. It represents a category which shares some common properties. Webster's Dictionary gives the word meaning of concept as a thought/opinion/philos, a mental image of the thing formed by a generalization from particulars, also an idea of what a thing in general is to be.

Concepts allow us to:

- differentiate various things or classes
- know relationship between objects
- generate ideas about events, things and processes

According to Bruner, a concept has five elements. They are:

- Name: It is the name or label given to a category. e.g. apple, orange, stars etc.
- Attributes: These refer to the characteristics of a particular concept that helps in distinguishing instances of the concept from non-instances. These attributes may be essential or non-essential. Essential attributes are the common features or characteristics of the concept. These attributes should be present in all the examples of the concept. Non-essential attributes are some of the slight differences among examples of a category.
- Examples: They refer to instances of concepts. There are positive and negative examples. Positive examples have all the essential attributes of the concept present in them. The non-essential attributes are present in some examples and absent in others. Bruner refers the examples, which contain the entire essential attribute as *positive* exemplars. The

absence of one or more essential attributes makes a *negative exemplar* of the concept. In concept formation, examples of a concept are grouped together. In concept attainment, the positive and negative examples are tested and searched for their features. The positive exemplars represent what the concept is. By arranging the exemplars sequentially, the student can reach a conclusion of what the concept is.

- Attribute value (attribute range): It refers to the acceptable range for any relevant attribute (essential attribute). This helps to distinguish the concept from super ordinate or coordinate concepts.
- The rule/definition: It is the definition or statement specifying the special attributes of a concept. A correct rule or statement is that reflects the successful utilization of the other elements of a concept.

When a learner can identify a positive exemplar of a concept from a negative exemplar on the basis of essential attributes, distinguish between essential and non-essential attributes in a positive exemplar of the concept and define the concept in terms of its attributes, we can say that the learner has attained the concept.

Variations of the Concept Attainment Model

There are three learning conditions of the concept attainment model. To facilitate the attainment of the concept there are three variations of the model:

- Reception model
- Selection model
- Unorganized material model

Reception Model

In the reception model of teaching concepts, the teacher presents his/her pupils an array of examples/instances. Some of these examples are positive and others are non-examples or negatives. The positive examples exemplify the concept and the negative examples do not. The teacher labels the former as 'YES' and the latter as 'NO'. The examples are generally presented by the teacher in general as one by one. At each encounter, the students compare the attributes of positive and negative examples and formulate and reformulate hypotheses regarding the concept. They are asked by the teacher to name the concept and state the rule/definition of the concepts according to its essential attributes. In case students find difficulty in naming the concept or stating the rule, the teacher extends help in this regard.

Then the teacher presents unlabelled examples and asks the students to label them as 'YES' or 'NO'. If the students are able to label the examples correctly, it manifests that they have attained the concept being taught to them. Students are thereafter asked to give a few examples to the concept on their own; it is an indicator that they have learnt the concept. The teacher then ask the learners to analyze the strategies through which they attained the concept. Some identify the common attributes in the first two positive examples and hypothesize in the light of attributes of positive and negative examples presented by the teacher. The teacher ask them what they did when their hypotheses were not confirmed. Students may be asked to compare the effectiveness of different strategies.

Selection Model

In the selection model, the teacher presents an array of examples. These examples are not marked as 'YES' or 'NO' as in the case of the reception model. The learner selects one unmarked examples and enquires whether it is a 'yes 'or 'no'. The major difference between the reception and selection model is in the labeling and sequencing of examples. Another difference is that the learners may ask about their own examples with a view to attaining the concept. In the selection model, there is a greater responsibility on the part of the learners to attain the concept than in the reception model. The model stimulates a greater level of thinking among learners.

Unorganized Materials Model

This mode of the concept attainment model is much more a group discussion than an instructional exercise as in the reception and selection modes. In this mode, the role of the teacher is to facilitate group discussion. In this model, learners attain concepts from unarranged materials. The procedure for attaining concept in this model involves the following steps:

- Locating the concepts

- Identifying the attributes
- Discussing the adequacy and appropriateness and adequacy of the attributes
- Comparing the examples to other instances using the concept.

Syntax

There are three phases in reception model of concept attainment. The activities in each phase are as follows. (Joyce and Weil, 1977).

Phases	Activities
Phase 1: Presentation of data and identification of concept	1. Teacher presents labelled examples 2. Students compare the attributes in positive and negative exemplars 3. Students generate and test hypotheses 4. Students state a definition according to the essential attributes
Phase II: Testing attainment of the concept	1. Students identify additional unlabelled examples as 'yes' or 'no' 2. Teacher confirms hypothesis, names concept and restates definition according to essential attributes 3. Students generate examples
Phase III: Analysis of thinking strategies	1. Students describe thoughts 2. Students discuss role of hypothesis and attributes 3. Students discuss types and number of hypotheses

In the first phase of the reception model, the teacher presents the positive and negative examples in the pre-determined sequence. This data may be in the form of pictures, anecdotes, sketches, diagrams, events or any other illustrations.

Pupils are told that there is one idea in common in all the positive examples and that they have to compare and justify the attributes and form some hypothesis about the concept.

When the pupils have analysed the examples and hypothesized, the teacher asks the students to state a definition according to the essential attribute.

In phase II, the teacher presents unlabelled examples. Pupils identify them as positive and negative. The teacher asks for reasons and confirms their hypothesis. When the teacher knows that the students have attained the concept, she names the concept. Only when the students have already attained the concept and the teacher uses the model for concept clarification and the teacher may ask the students to name the concept.

To test the attainment of the concept further, the teacher asks the pupils to generate examples and label them as positive and negative instances of the concept.

In the third phase of the model, the teacher analyses the thinking strategies employed by the students. The students report their pattern of hypothesizing, whether they focused on attributes or concepts, whether they did so one at a time or several at once and how they changed their hypothesis when it was not confirmed.

Social System: The model has a moderate structure. The teacher assumes a major role initially in choosing the concept, selecting and organising or sequencing the data. The teacher controls action, but with subsequent phases, the student interaction is encouraged.

Principles of Reaction: The model emphsises teacher support during the flow of the lesson. Pupils should be helped in creating a dialogue in which students test their hypothesis against each other. The teacher should focus pupil's attention on specific features of examples and finally assists the pupils, in discussing and evaluating their thinking strategies. The teacher should encourage analysis of the merits of various strategies rather than attempting to seek the one best strategy for all pupils in all situations.

Support System

It requires materials in the form of examples marked as '+ve' or '–ve'. To be presented to the students for concept attainment. These may be presented as real objects, or in the form of pictures, sketches, diagrams, events or any other illustrations.

Effects of the Model

The concept attainment model accomplishes several instructional effects depending on the emphasis of the particular lesson. They are:

1. Understanding of the nature of concept
2. Specific concepts
3. Improved concept building strategies
4. Inductive reasoning ability

The nurturant effects come from experiencing the environment created by the model. These effects are:

1. Awareness of alternative perspectives
2. Tolerance of ambiguity (but appreciation of logic)
3. Sensitivity to logical reasoning in communication.

LESSON PLAN
USING CONCEPT ATTAINMENT MODEL

Subject: Physics
Standard: IX
Model: Concept attainment

Unit : Motion
Topic: Circular motion

Objectives

The students

- recognize the attributes of the concept, circular motion correctly
- state the attributes correctly
- label the unlabelled examples given by the teacher correctly
- generate new examples of concepts
- formulate concept and rule
- locate the examples and state attributes of the concept as appeared in the example

Type of Model: Reception strategies
The Learning Modality: Experiments and examples

Elements of the Concept

Name: Circular motion

Essential Attributes:
i) Objects which are travelling along a circular path have uniform speed.
ii) The direction of motion along a circular path always changes.
iii) The direction of motion is along the tangent to the circular path.

Non-essential Attributes:
i) Rotation of earth around the sun
ii) Spin motion of earth.

Positive examples:
i) Motion of cycle wheel

ii) Revolving of artificial satellites
iii) Rotation of earth

Negative Examples:
i) Motion of waves
ii) Bouncing of rubber ball
iii) Motion of cycle along straight road
iv) Motion of simple pendulum

Rule: Motion along a circular path

Phase I: Presentation of Data and Identification of the Concept

Teacher- Pupil activities	Strategies
Teacher: Today we are going to play a game. I will give you some examples of a particular concept. If the examples contain the concept, I will say, it is an 'Yes' example. If the example does not contain the concept, I will say, it is a 'No' example. You should say what that particular concept which is in my mind. You should cite more examples and form a definition of that concept according to the characteristics. Now let us see an 'Yes' example.' Motion of earth around the sun'. Can you say what the concept is? **Students:** No. Please give more examples. **Teacher:** Let's pass to the second example, which is an 'Yes'. 'Revolution of artificial satellite'. **Students:** Can you give another example? **Teacher;** Rotation of earth. It is an 'Yes' example. **Students:** These motions are along the circular path. **Teacher;** Good. I shall give you 'No' examples. 'To and fro motion of a person sitting in a swing', 'Bouncing of a rubber ball' and motion of waves. These are 'no' examples. **Students:** There are differences in the direction of motion in the above two sets of examples. **Teacher:** Have you got the concepts presented in 'Yes' examples? **Students:** No. **Teacher:** What differences in the direction of motion, you can see in these two sets of examples? **Students:** the motion is around a circular path in the first set of examples. **Teacher:** Good. You have got the concept. What term we can use to denote such type of motions? **Students:** Can we use the term circular motion? **Teacher;** Yes. The motion of an object along the circular path is known as circular motion.	Orientation to the process Teacher presents the first labelled example. Teacher presents more labelled examples. Teacher presents unlabelled examples. Students formulate the first hypothesis. Students name the concept as circular motion. Teacher states the concept rule.

Phase II: Testing the Attainment of the Concept

Teacher: Now, I would like to know whether you have understood the concept. I shall give you some instances. You have to say that whether these are 'Yes' or 'No' examples for circular motion.	Teacher presents unlabelled examples.
i) Rotation of earth. **Students:** It is an 'Yes' example for circular motion. **Teacher:** Correct. Another one. "Motion of cycle along a straight road". **Students:** No. It is a 'No' example for circular motion. **Teacher:** Now, Can you give an 'Yes' example for circular motion? **Students:** motion of a cycle wheel. **Teacher:** Correct. Can you give a 'No' example for circular motion. **Students:** Motion of simple pendulum.	Students label unlabelled examples. Students cite more examples.

Phase III: Analysis of Thinking Strategies

Teacher: Can you explain how did you arrive at the concept? **Students:** When you presented two 'Yes' examples, it was difficult to form the concepts. When we saw the motion of cycle wheel we found that, the motion of the wheel is around the circular path. When we saw the motion of simple pendulum we found that the motion is different from the motion we observed in the first example. When you give the example of revolving of satellites, we got the real idea about circular motion. When the 'No' example, the motion of cycle along straight line is given, it became easy to identify the characteristics of circular motion.	Students describe thought process

Consolidation

Circular motion is rotation along a circle: The path or orbit of such motion is circular.

The circular motion can be uniform or non-uniform.

Examples of circular motion—

1. an artificial satellite orbiting the Earth in geosynchronous orbit
2. a stone which is tied to a rope and is being swung in circles
3. a racecar turning through a curve in a race track
4. an electron moving perpendicular to a uniform magnetic field
5. a gear turning inside a mechanism.

In Circular motion the angular rate of rotation is constant, though it is accelerated as the direction of motion always changed. Due to such change in direction of velocity involves acceleration of the moving object by a centripetal force, which pulls the moving object toward the center of the circular orbit. Without this acceleration, the object would move in a straight line.

INQUIRY TRAINING MODEL (ITM)

Inquiry training model belongs to the information processing family of models. It was developed by Richard Suchman. This model attempts to teach students the process of investigating and explaining unusual phenomena. Based on the conception of scientific method, it attempts to teach students, some of the skills and the language of inquiry. The basic assumptions behind this model are:

1. Students inquire naturally when they are puzzled.
2. They can become conscious of and learn to analyse their thinking strategies.
3. New strategies can be taught directly and added to the student's existing ones.
4. Cooperative inquiry enriches thinking and help students to learn about the tentative and emerging nature of knowledge and alternative explanations.

The specific objectives of ITM are:

1. To develop science process skills-observing, collecting and organising data, identifying and controlling variables, formulating and testing hypotheses, and the ability to explain and infer
2. To develop among students the strategies for creative inquiry.

Apart from these main objectives there are some subsidiary objectives. These are:

i. To develop among students an independence or autonomy in learning.
ii. To develop among students the ability to tolerate ambiguity.
iii. To make the students understand the tentative nature of knowledge.

Description of the Model

Synatx: The following are the phases of inquiry.

Phase	Activity
Phase I: Encounter with the problem	The teacher presents the preplanned discrepant event and explains the inquiry procedure
Phase II: Data gathering verification	The students inquire about the nature and identity of objects, events, properties and conditions related to the problem.
Phase III: Data gathering experimentation	Asks the students to organize the data which they have gathered and to give the most appropriate explanation which fits the data. (causal relationship, isolating variables)
Phase IV: Formulating rules or explanations	Teacher asks the pupils to formulate rules based on the phase III
Phase V: Analysis of the inquiry process	Asks the students to analyze their pattern of inquiry

Social System: The teacher selects or designs the puzzling situations and presents it to the students. However, during the inquiry session teachers and students participates as equals. As the students learn the principles of inquiry, the teacher guides them, in the use of resources, materials, perform experiments and conduct discussion with other students.

Principles of Reaction: Ensure that the phrasing of the question eliciting 'Yes' or 'No' answer is done correctly. If the teacher is asked questions that cannot be answered by 'Yes' or 'No', she must ask the students to rephrase the questions. Make sure that there are no repetitions. Ask the students to make clear statements of theories and provide support for their generalizations. Encourage interactions.

Support System: All the specific conditions required for the smooth running of all phases of the model is called support system. These would include books, films, posters and apparatuses required for experimentation.

Instructional and Nurturant Effects

Instructional Effects: The instructional effects of inquiry training model are:

1. Scientific process
2. Strategies for creative inquiry

Nurturant Effects: the nurturant effects are:

1. Spirit of creativity
2. Independence of autonomy in learning
3. Tolerance of ambiguity
4. Tentative nature of knowledge

LESSON PLAN BASED ON INQUIRY TRAINING MODEL

Topic: The Electrical conductivity of acids

Objectives

1. Students will be able to formulate an explanation of the floating of substances in water.
2. They will be able to develop process skills like observing, experimenting, organising data, formulating and testing hypothesis and drawing inference.
3. They will be engaged in strategies for creative inquiry through questioning.

Support System

In order to present the problem to the students, the teacher uses basin, water, coins, cork, clip, small plastic bowls, glass bowls and spoons.

Phase I: Presentation of the Problem and Explanation of the Inquiry Process

Teacher presents the discrepant event as follows: students in the class visited shipyard at Cochin. They saw a number of ships in the sea. They came to know that ship is made up of iron and it does not sink in the water. But a hair pin made by iron put in the water sinks. The teacher made it to the notice of students and they are interested in making an inquiry regarding this. Here teacher starts the inquiry process in the form of a game. The teacher presents the inquiry procedure which the students should follow. She says:

In order to solve the problem, you have to find out facts pertaining to the problem. You can ask a series of questions. But the questions you ask have to be framed in such a way that the answer to them has to be just 'Yes' or 'No'. If the question does not elicit either answer, you have to rephrase it.

Phase II and III: Data Gathering Experimentation and Verification

The pupils ask fact finding questions.

PUPIL: Is the same material used for constructing the ship and the hair pin?

TEACHER: Yes.

PUPIL: Is the small size of the clip instrumental to its immersion?

TEACHER: No.

Teacher provides some materials like a large basin with water, coins, cork, clip, small plastic bowls, glass bowls, spoons etc. Students perform experiments with the materials and came to know that the size or shape is not the reason for its immersion.

PUPIL: Is two forces are acted upon the body when it is immersed?

TEACHER: Yes.

Pupil: Does the force exerted by the hair pin on seawater is equal to the weight of the pin?

TEACHER: Yes.

PUPIL: Does the sea water exert any opposite force on the hair pin?

TEACHER: Yes

PUPIL: Is not the force the buoyant force?

TEACHER: Yes

PUPIL: Does the body get immersed when its weight is greater than the buoyant force?

TEACHER: Yes.

PUPIL: What will happen if the buoyant force is greater than the weight of the body/

TEACHER: Not a proper question. Please rephrase it.

PUPIL: Does the body float when the buoyant force is greater than the weight of the body?

TEACHER: Yes.

PUPIL: Does the sea water exert different buoyant force on different objects?

TEACHER: No

PUPIL: Does a body displace some quantity of liquid when it is immersed?

TEACHER: Yes

PUPIL: Is there any relationship between the weight of the body and the weight of the liquid displaced by the body?

TEACHER: Yes

PUPIL: What happens when the weight of the water displaced is less than that the weight of the body?

TEACHER: Not a proper question. Please rephrase it.

PUPIL: Does the body get immersed if the weight of the liquid displaced is less than the weight of the body?

TEACHER: Yes.

PUPIL: does the ship displace water?

TEACHER: Yes

PUPIL: Does the greater volume of ship cause an increase in the volume of water displaced?

TEACHER: Yes

PUPIL: Is this the reason for the floating of ship?

TEACHER: Yes

PUPIL: Is the lesser volume of water displaced by the hair pin and correspondingly the lesser buoyant force is responsible for the sinking of hair pin?

TEACHER: Yes.

Phase IV: Formulation of an Explanation

Teacher : You have noted that the greater volume of ship cause an increase in volume of water displaced by the ship is the reason for floating of the ship and the lesser volume of water displaced by the hair pin cause it sinking. Then what can you infer from this?

Pupil: So a body gets immersed in liquids if the weight of liquid displaced by the body is less than the weight of the body.

Teacher: Yes. A body gets immersed in liquids if the weight of liquid displaced by the body is less than the weight of the body. And a body floats in the liquid if the weight of liquid displaced by the body is greater than the weight of the body.

Phase V: Analysis of the Inquiry Process

Teacher: How did you find that the body gets immersed in liquids if the weight of liquid displaced by the body is less than the weight of the body? And the body floats in the liquid if the weight of liquid displaced by the body is greater than the weight of the body?

Pupil: When we find that the two objects are made up of same materials and the size or weight of the bodies are not relevant here, we came to notice that, the difference in force they exert on the water may be the cause. Then we found that water also exerts a force back and it is the buoyant force. Then we found that the buoyant force in the case of ship is very large since it replaces a large quantity of water. Then we hypothesize that if the buoyant force is greater than the weight of the ship, then it will float on the water surface. When you confirmed our doubts, it was verified.

7E LEARNING MODEL

The learning cycle model of instruction, was originally proposed by Atkin and Karplus (1962). It was used as the instructional bases for the 'Science Curriculum improvement study programme' by Karplus and Their (1967). It is based on Piagetian theory and involves a constructivist approach to teaching. It is intended to help students progress from concrete to abstract thinking about content. Learning cycles teach science in three consecutive phases known as exploration, term introduction, and concept application that are based on the way people spontaneously learn about the world. These phases have been described as follows: Exploration allows students to investigate new materials and/or ideas so that patterns of regularity can be discovered and questions are raised that students then attempt to answer. Term introduction allows the teacher to introduce terms to label the patterns and to explain the newly invented concepts. Concept application provokes students to seek the patterns elsewhere and to apply the new concepts to additional examples, often employing abstraction or generalization techniques (Lawson, 1989). Research has supported the effectiveness of the learning cycle in encouraging students to think creatively and critically, as well as in facilitating a better understanding of scientific concepts, developing positive attitudes toward science, improving science process skills, and cultivating advanced reasoning skills.

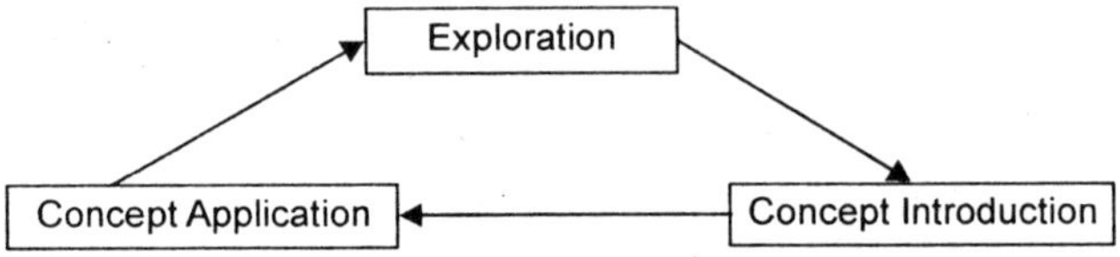

Fig. 6.1: Learning Cycle of Science Curriculum Improvement Study

As an instructional approach, the origin of the learning cycle is generally attributed to the Science Curriculum Improvement Study (SCIS) materials of the 1970s. Many versions of the learning cycle appear in science curricula with phases ranging in number from three to five (5Es) to seven (7Es).

The *5E learning cycle* based instruction was developed by the Biological Sciences Curriculum Study (BSCS) in 1989. It consists of 5 phases called as; Engagement, Exploration, Explanation, Elaboration and Evaluation.

Another version of learning cycle is *7E model (elicit, engage, explore, explain, elaborate, evaluate, and extend).* Research on how people learn and the incorporation of that research into lesson plans and curriculum development demanded that the 5E model to be expanded to a 7E model. The proposed 7E model expands the engage phase in the 5E model into two components—elicit and engage. Similarly, the 7E model expands the two stages of elaborate and evaluates into three components—elaborate, evaluate, and extend. Table below shows the comparison of the 5E and 7E learning cycles.

The addition of the extend phase to the elaborate phase is intended to explicitly remind teachers of the importance for students to practice the transfer of learning. Teachers need to make sure that knowledge is applied in a new context and is not limited to simple elaboration. The goal of the 7E learning model is to emphasize the increasing importance of eliciting prior understanding and the extending, or transfer of concepts. With this new model, teachers should no longer overlook these essential requirements for student learning (Eisenkraft, 2003).

Whether the instruction have three phases, five phases or seven phases, the teacher should design a learning cycle to reveal prior knowledge, to show that students' misconceptions are not suitable for explaining scientific concepts and to let the students see that these new concepts are intelligible, plausible and fruitful.

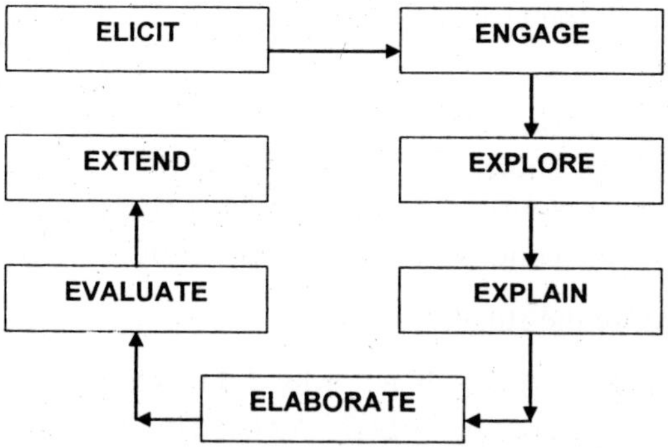

Fig. 6.2: 7E Learning Cycle

The learning cycle is a model for designing science lessons to foster successful, positive experiences for students. The 7 E learning cycle constitutes seven phases in the teaching learning strategy.

- Elicit
- Engage
- Explore
- Explain
- Elaboration
- Extend
- Evaluate

Phase 1: Elicit

The purpose of the Elicit phase is the determination of the prior conceptions: "what do you know about...?". This phase might involve a "student talk", discussion of some aspect of the content. This phase might be addressed through the process of interviewing selected students about their background knowledge of the key ideas of the lesson.

Phase 2: Engagement

In this phase, activities that initiate students' curiosity are made. These activities help students to make connections with the previous knowledge. The Engage phase is intended to motivate students, to capture their interest in the topic. Interest can be captured in many ways, for example through a discrepant event, demonstration, an interesting natural or human made object, a challenging question, or a problem to solve.

In this stage the teacher:

- creates interest
- creates curiosity
- raises questions
- elicits responses that uncover what students know or think about the concept (Carin & Bass, 2000)

In this stage the student:

- asks questions such as: "why did this happen?", "what do i already know about this?", "what can i find out about this?"
- shows interest in the topic. (Carin & Bass, 2000)

Phase3: Exploration

Once students are engaged in the learning tasks, exploration activities follow. In exploration, students observe properties, form simple relationships, note patterns and raise questions about events to develop fundamental awareness of the nature of materials and ideas. They have the opportunity to get directly involved with phenomena. The teacher's role in the exploration phase is that of guide, coach and facilitator.

In this stage the teacher:

- encourages students to work without direct instruction from the teacher.
- observes and listens to students as they interact.
- asks probing questions to redirect students' investigations when necessary.
- provides time for students' investigations when necessary.
- provides time for students to puzzle through problems.
- acts as a consultant for students. (Carin & Bass, 2000)

In this stage the student:

- thinks freely, but within the limits of the activity.
- tests predictions and hypotheses.
- forms new predictions and hypotheses.
- tries alternatives and discusses them with others.
- records observations and ideas.
- suspends judgment. (Carin & Bass, 2000)

Phase 4: Explanation

In this phase, teachers help students make sense of their observations and answer the questions that arise from their observations. The teacher asks children to describe what they see and give their own explanations of why it happened. Then, the teacher introduced a scientific explanation for the event through formal and direct instruction. The teacher connected the scientific explanation with the physical evidence from exploration and engagement and relates it to the explanations that the children have formed. Verbal methods are most common here, but the teacher might also use videos, books, multimedia presentations, and computer courseware.

In this stage the teacher:

- Encourages students to explain concepts and definitions in their own words
- Asks for justification (evidence) and clarification from students
- Formally provides definitions, explanations and new labels
- Uses students' previous experience as the basis for explaining concepts (Carin & Bass, 2000)

In this stage the student:

- Explains possible solutions or answers to the others
- Listens critically to one another's explanations
- Questions one another's explanations
- Listens to and tries to comprehend explanations offered by the teacher
- Refers to previous activities
- Uses recorded observations in explanations (Carin & Bass, 2000)

Phase 5: Elaboration

In this phase, new experiences are designed to assist children in developing broader understandings of the concepts already introduced. Students expand on the concepts they have learned, make connections to other related concepts, and apply their understanding to the real world around them. Children work in cooperative groups, identify and complete new activities. It often involves experimental inquiry, investigative projects, problem solving and decision making. Lab work is common. Small-group and whole-class discussions provide students, the opportunities to present their own understandings. By observing the students in this phase, the teacher may decide to recycle through the different phases of the 7E learning cycle to improve the children's understanding or move on to new science lessons.

In this stage the teacher:

- expects students to use formal labels, definitions, and explanations provided previously
- encourages students to apply or extend the concepts and skills in new situations
- reminds students of alternative explanations
- refers students to existing data and evidence and asks: "What do you already know?" "Why do you think...?" (Carin & Bass, 2000)

In this stage the student:

- applies new labels, definitions, explanations, and skills in new, but similar situations
- uses previous information to ask questions, propose solutions, and make decisions, design experiments
- draws reasonable conclusions from evidence
- records reasonable conclusions from evidence
- records observations and explanations
- checks for understanding among peers (Carin & Bass, 2000)

Phase 6: Extend

The purpose of this phase is to provide for the transfer of the new concepts to different contexts. This phase challenges student's understandings to apply what they have learned.

Phase 7: Evaluation

Evaluation and assessment occurs at all points along the continuum of the instructional process. Rubrics, teacher observation structured by checklists, student interviews, portfolios designed with specific purposes, project and problem-based learning products, concept maps and roundhouse diagrams may be used to assess students' understanding of concepts. By using this tool, the teacher can detect students' misconceptions and correct the inaccurate conclusions. Roundhouse diagrams may be used as a tool in the evaluation part. By using these tools, teachers observe students as they apply new concepts and skills to assess students' knowledge and/or skills, looking for evidence that the students have changed their thinking or behaviours. The opportunity to allow students to assess their own learning and group-process skills is often provided.

In this stage the teacher:

- observe students as they apply new concepts and skills
- assesses students' knowledge and/or skills
- looks for evidence that students have changed their thinking or behaviours
- allows students to assess their own learning and group process skills
- asks open-ended questions, such as: "Why do you think....?", "What evidence do you have?", "What do you know about x?" How would you explain x?" (Carin & Bass, 2000)

In this stage the student:

- answers open-ended questions by using observations, evidences, and previously accepted explanations
- demonstrates an understanding or knowledge of the concept or skill

LESSON PLAN
BASED ON 7E LEARNING CYCLE

Standard: IX *Unit*: Fluids
Topic: Viscous Force *Time*: 45'
Link to Previous Lessons: Fluids, Frictional force
Pre-requisite objectives: Students should have knowledge about fluids, friction and properties of frictional force.

General Objectives

At the end, the students will

- acquire knowledge about frictional force

- developing understanding about the force which oppose motion of fluids
- apply the knowledge while handling fluids which we use in daily life
- develop skill in doing simple experiments
- develop scientific attitude through the study of viscous
- develop interest in observing the nature and properties of viscous force

Specific Objectives

At the end force of the lesson then students will be able to:

- recall frictional force
- illustrate viscosity of different liquids
- compare the viscosity of different liquids
- identify the relationship between viscosity and temperature
- discriminate between viscous liquids and mobile liquids
- cite examples for viscous liquids and mobile liquids
- raise questions about viscosity
- formulate operational definition for viscosity
- design simple experiments to compare viscosity of different fluids
- see the relationship between frictional force and viscous force
- synthesise ideas regarding viscosity
- show eagerness to know more about viscous force
- develop self confidence
- develop team spirit
- gives multiple responses for how to compare viscosity

Instructional Materials

Work sheet, black board, concept map, glass plates, 200 ml. of honey, 200 ml. of alcohol, 200 ml. of coloured water, 200 ml. of kerosene, 200 ml. of coconut oil.

Teaching Strategy

7E learning cycle

Pre-assignment

Students should revise the topics—friction and frictional force

Post-assignments

Students will be given problems to be solved related to 'viscous force'. Also they should prepare their concept map on viscous force.

Preparation of Students

At the beginning of the lesson, concepts on friction and frictional force will be revised. The main purpose here is to bring the relevant prior knowledge to the students' mind. Students discuss their guess and hypotheses with their peers and find out suitable solutions.

Preparation of the Teacher

1. Preparation of concept maps
2. Preparation for conducting experiments
3. Preparation of questions for group discussion
4. Preparation of work sheets

Cues, Feedback, Reinforcement and Motivation

When a correct answer is given by students, the teacher will give positive verbal reinforcement. Students will be encouraged to participate in the lesson. The feedback and cues will be given for concept maps and work sheets.

Presentation of the Topic with the Learning Cycle Model

1. Elicitation

The teacher will create groups of four students. Each group will be given concept map related to molecular forces. In this stage, students' prior conceptions will be tried to be identified.

2. Engagement

The teacher will start lesson by questioning daily life examples.

- Why, we are using gum to stick some materials?
- Why the rain drops have such a spherical shape?
- The small quantities of mercury placed on a clean glass plate should have spherical shape why?

Then the teacher will make a demonstration, she will take a wire ring and dip it in a soap solution. That thin film is placed with a moistened cotton loop. And then, she will prick on the film inside the loop by a pin. The students will observe the experiment, and then the teacher will ask the following questions.

- What do you think about the following situations?
- The cotton loop will remain in any form or position in which it is placed, because........
- When pricked the film, the loop inside the cotton will disappear, because ......
- The film has a tendency to contract or shrink because.........

The teacher will create groups of four students and she will allow students 5-7 minutes to think about the questions individually and then share it with their groups. And also discuss the terms, with the clues given by the teacher.

- Molecular range.
- Sphere of influence
- Cohesive presence,
- Surface film and
- Surface energy.

In this stage teacher will generate curiosity in the topic of study, and raise questions and elicit responses from students that will give an idea of what they already know.

3. Exploration

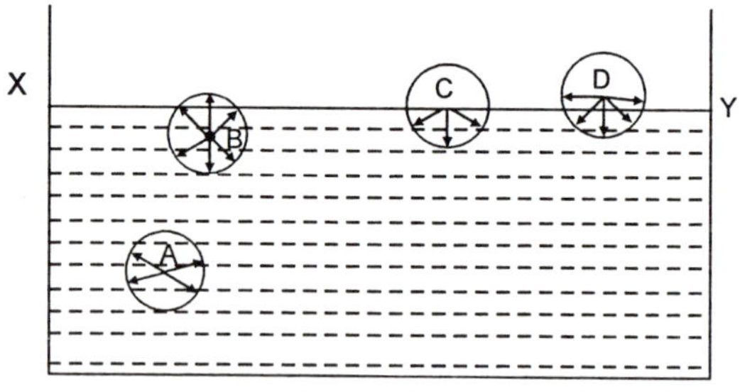

Fig. 6.3: Force Acting on Molecules in a Liquid

The teacher will give some worksheet with this picture; it will help the students to find out the reason behind surface tension.

- Teacher will ask some questions, related to the sphere of influence of the liquid spheres, A, B, C and D.

- Asking questions about the resultant force, its cohesive force.
- Asking questions about the presence of thermal velocity.
- Teacher will ask questions to the students to reveal the idea of surface film and also related to the energy—i.e. surface energy.

During the discussion, the students will have opportunity to express their ideas and see their peer's thoughts. In this stage the purpose of the teacher is to let the student manipulates materials to actively explore concepts, processes or skills. The teacher will be the facilitator and observe and listen to students as they interact.

4. Explanation

The teacher will listen to each group's answer. Then, she will explain the concept using student's previous experiences.

Molecular Range and Sphere of Influence

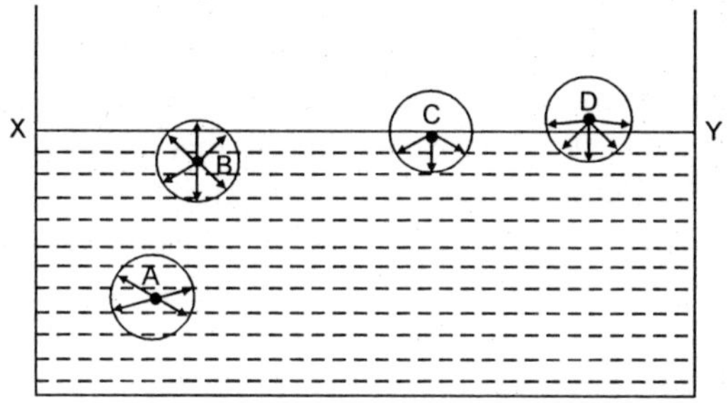

Fig. 6.4: Force Acting on Molecules in a Liquid

The greatest distance at which the molecules can attract each other is called their molecular range. A sphere drawn with the molecule as centre and molecular range as radius is called the sphere of influence.

A molecule attracts and is attracted by all the molecules lying within its sphere of influence, while for the molecules beyond it, the attraction is inappreciable as it varies inversely at some high power of the distance. The molecular range for solids and liquids is of the order of 10^{-7} cm, being different for different substances. Under ordinary conditions of temperature and pressure, the molecules of a gas are very far apart, so that the force of cohesion in gases in almost negligible.

Cohesive Pressure, Surface Film and Surface Energy

Consider XY, a free surface of a liquid and let there be four molecules of the liquid, 'A' well within the liquid, 'B' just below the surface, 'C' on the surface and 'D' just above the surface, each molecule with its sphere of influence drawn around it. As the sphere of influence of 'A' lies wholly within the liquid, it is equally attracted from all sides so that there is no resultant cohesive force acting upon it and the molecule is free to move about in all directions.

In the case of the molecules 'B', a part of the upper hemisphere of its sphere of influence lies outside the liquid so that the number of molecules in the upper hemisphere of its sphere of influence is less than those in the lower hemisphere. Thus the cohesive force exerted on it by the molecules in the upper hemisphere is less than that exerted by the molecules in the lower hemisphere. Hence there is resultant downward cohesive force acting upon the molecule 'B'.

The molecule 'C' lies on the surface so that its sphere of influence is exactly half outside the liquid and half inside it, and hence it is attracted inward with the maximum cohesive force acting to the surface.

The molecule 'D' lie on the surface so that its sphere of influence lying inside the liquid, the force of attraction inward decreases and when its sphere of influence goes entirely outside the liquid surface, the molecule is no longer under the action of any inward force. Thus we see that all over the liquid surface' there is an inward pull due to the attraction of molecules. This inward force exerted on a unit area of the liquid surface is called the cohesive pressure or internal pressure.

Obviously molecules of the liquid is the surface film as under a downward cohesive force which increases as the free surface of the liquid which appears to have a 'skin'.

If a molecule is taken from within the liquid to the surface film, work has to be done against the downward cohesive force and this increases its potential energy. Thus the potential energy of the molecules lying within the surface film is greater than the potential energy of the molecules lying within the liquid. Now the system is in stable equilibrium when its potential energy is minimum so that the surface film tends to have the least possible area and the minimum number of molecules, as its thickness is fixed.

The potential energy per unit area of the surface is called its surface energy. Thus for a given volume of the liquid not in contact with solids its free surface will always tend to alter the shape of its surface so as to have the minimum surface area. This is the fundamental property of every liquid and exhibits itself in many ways.

5. Elaboration

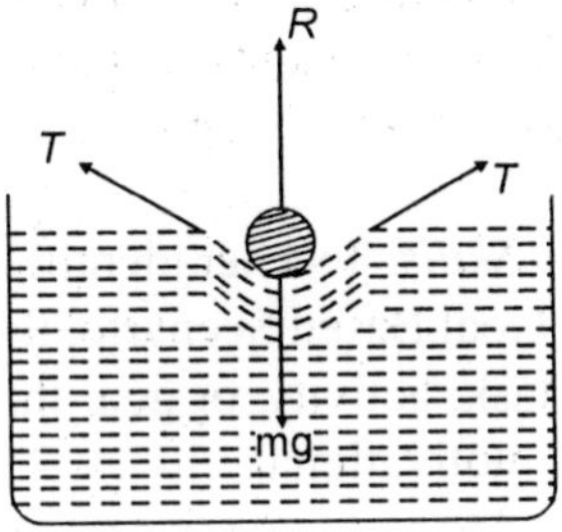

Fig. 6.5: Surface Energy on a Liquid Drop

Floating Needle

The teacher will distribute the picture above to the students; have then discussed what the reason behind it is.

6. Extension

Take a camel hair pain brush and dip it into water. Its hair gets separated from water. Then take the brush out of water. Its hair will ding together as a free surface of water films try to contract. The teacher will give this topic to the group. The students will discuss about it.

7. Evaluation

- The teachers will summarise the topic with the help of students.
- Teacher will ask some review questions in this stage.
- As a part of extension, teacher will give some arrangements related to this topic.
- Then the teacher will create groups of four students. Each group will be given concept map related to the topic surface tension and surface energy. Also students will be given questions and their questions will be discussed together.

GOAL BASED SCENARIO MODEL

A Goal Based Scenario is a learn-by-doing simulation, proposed by R.C. Schank (1994). Schank defined Goal Based Scenario as the "natural learning goals that have to do with increased understanding or increasing one's power to operate successfully in various endeavors to get replaced by artificial learning goals that have to do with acceptance, approval and socialization". Students should learn to apply certain skills in authentic contexts that relate to their interests. The following essential components of Goal Based Scenario form the phases of Goal Based Scenario Model.

- *Identify Target Skills:* Teacher identifies a specific set of skills to teach via a Goal Based Scenario, then embedded that skill learning in a task, activity, or goal that the student will find interesting or motivational.
- *Developing a Mission:* A mission is something a student achieves by applying any number of skills. In other words, a mission is a state or condition.
- *The Focus of a Goal Based Scenario:* The focus of a Goal Based Scenario specifies what general class of task the student will learn through the Goal Based Scenario. Choose a general class of skills the student will learn.
  - Design—create an artifact
  - Diagnosis—analyze or explain problems faced by a group
  - Discovery—apply techniques or strategies from one group to another
  - Control—Manage simulated setting
- *Create a Cover Story for the Mission:* The cover story establishes the context of a Goal Based Scenario. The cover story defines the premise under which the student pursues the mission. It lays out the scenes where the action takes place and other details that flesh out the Goal Based Scenario making it more plausible and enticing to the student.
- *The Operations of a Goal Based Scenario:* the operations specify the concrete activities. It contains specific for students in a Goal Based Scenario. Operations might include actions such as:
  - Issuing a directive in a social simulation
  - Answering a question
  - Using a tool to shape part of an artifact
  - Searching for a piece of information

- *Resources:* Resources provide the information the students need to achieve the goal of the mission.
- *Feedback:* A way that allows learners to properly index information as it is given. The feedback can be given in any of three ways.
  - The consequence of actions
  - Through coaches
  - Through domain experts

Goal Based Scenario constitutes an alternative to traditional intelligent tutoring systems that combine elements of simulation, case-based reasoning and traditional tutoring systems modelling techniques. It helps the students learn certain cognitive skills in authentic contexts that relate to their interests. Therefore the investigator thought that it will be helpful to enhance science process skills among students.

LESSON PLAN BASED ON GOAL BASED SCENARIO MODEL

Name of the Teacher: Vandana Ghosh *Subject*: Physics
Name of the School: St. Mary's G.H.S. Kuravilangad
Unit: Electricity Class: IX
Topic: Current *Time*: 45 minutes

Content Overview

Current—Parts of a used cell—identify the devices used in the circuit

Content Analysis

Term

- Current

Facts

- Flow of electrons is considered as electric current.
- Electric current flows from the point where electric pressure or potential is higher to a point where it is low.
- Potential difference has to be maintained between the ends of a conductor if a current is to flow continuously through it.

Concepts

- *Electric Current*: The amount of charge that flows through a circuit in one second is called electric current.
- *Potential Difference*: If an electric current is to flow between two points of a conductor, one of the points should be at a higher energy level. This difference of potential between the two points is called potential difference.

Specific Objectives

After learning this lesson, the students will be able to

- formulate hypothesis
- evaluate hypothesis
- develop skill of experimenting
- recognize the observed facts
- draw inferences from observed facts

Pre and Misconception

Students have an idea about electric current.

Instructional Materials

Worksheets, beaker, dilute sulphuric acid, zinc plate and copper plate.

Teaching Strategy

Goal Based Scenario Model.

Phase I: Identify Target Skill

Teacher wants to develop the skill of evaluating hypothesis and drawing inferences related to the topic current and potential difference.

Phase II: Developing a Mission

Here students try to construct the voltaic cell.

Phase III: Choose a Focus

Teacher chooses an appropriate focus for students to reach the mission. Here students are asked to control and manage the experimental settings related to the topic voltaic cell.

Phase IV: Create a Cover Story for the Mission

One day Deepu went out with his father for a walk. He asked a question to his father while seeing a lake "Dad, why does water flows from a higher place to a lower place? And how is it that electricity flows from the bottom to the top"?

Phase V: Plan the Operations

TEACHER: Didn't you notice the battery used in a car? From where did we get the power to start a car?

PUPIL: Battery

TEACHER: Did you notice the battery of your mobile phone? What about the volt of your mobile phone battery?

TEACHER: Did you hear about cell? What is cell? What is the difference between cell and battery? Let's do an experiment related to the production of electricity.

Activity I

Teacher provides a beaker, dilute sulphuric acid, zinc plate, copper plate galvanometer and copper wire to each group to make a cell. Then the teacher gives instructions to them.

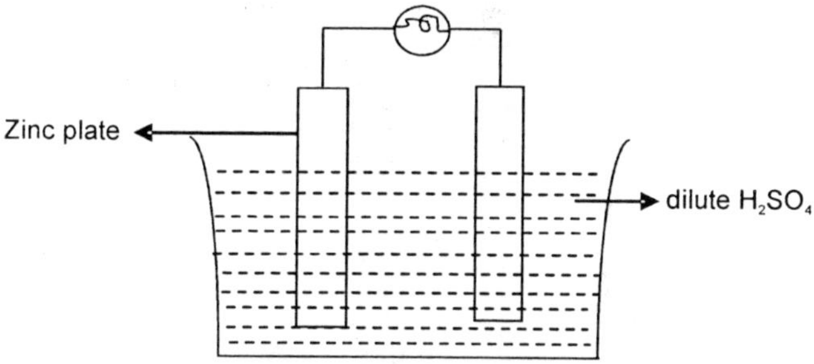

Fig. 6.6: Electric Cell

Make the arrangements as shown in the figure. Fill three fourth of a breaker with dilute sulphuric acid and take a zinc plate and a copper plate. Connect them to a galvanometer. Observe the galvanometer reading. Now dip these plates in the acid without mutual contact. What change in the reading of the galvanometer do you observe?

Worksheet

- What did you observe in this activity?
- Which is the plate on which bubbles are formed?
- Why are the bubbles maintain as such?

- What is the form of energy that maintains the potential difference throughout here?

Group Discussion

Each group discusses their ideas in the class room and form a general conclusion with the help of teacher.

Idea to be Consolidated

Cell is another source of Electro Motive Force. Chemical reaction produces electricity and it flows from positive terminal to negative terminal.

Activity II

Teacher provides a used cell to each group for doing the next activity and gives instructions to identify the parts of a cell.

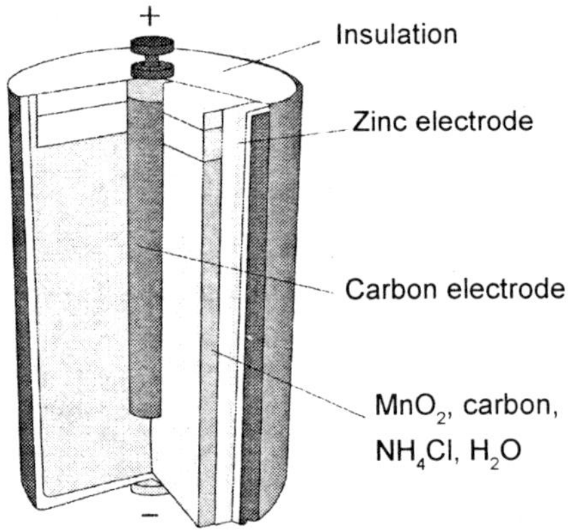

Fig. 6.7: Dry Cell

Group Discussion

Each group discusses their finding about the parts of a dry cell and forms a general conclusion.

Idea to be Consolidated

A cell has two terminals—a positive and a negative terminal. Positive terminal is anode and negative is cathode.

Activity III

The teacher provides a voltmeter, a bulb, an ammeter, key and a battery to each group to make the connections as shown in the figure.

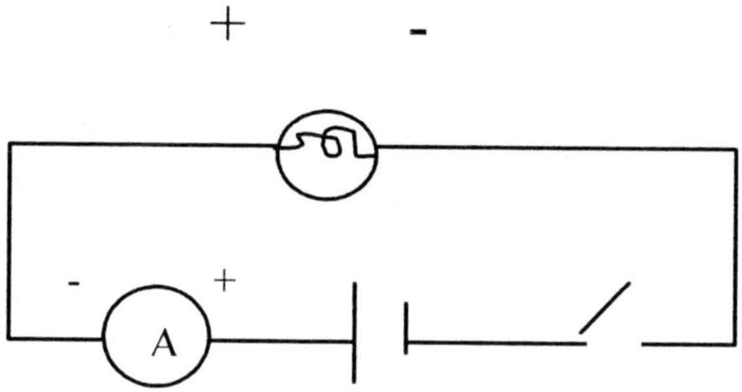

Fig. 6.8: Electric Circuit

Worksheet

- List the devices used in the circuit?
- What is the need of each of these devices?
- How much current flows through a circuit, if a charge of 6C flows through it in 10 second?

Group Discussion

Each group discusses their findings with other group and formulates a generalization with the help of teacher.

Idea to be Consolidated

Voltmeter, ammeter, bulb, cell, and key are the devices used in the circuit.

Phase VI: Resources

The supporting materials are voltmeter, ammeter, cell, bulb, beaker, sulphuric acid, zinc plate, copper plate and galvanometer.

Phase VII: Feed Back

Teacher evaluates the performance of each group and gives necessary suggestions and modifications to them.

WORK SHEET

Name of the School	:	Class : IX D
Group No.	:	Date : 13/12/2010
Name of the Group Members	:	Period :
		Subject : Physics
		Unit :
		Topic : Current.

Activity I

1. ഈ പ്രവർത്തനത്തിൽ കുമിളകൾ ഉണ്ടാകുന്നു.
2. കോപ്പർ പ്ലേറ്റിൽ കുമിളകൾ ഉണ്ടാകുന്നു.
3. രാസപ്രവർത്തനം നടക്കുന്നതുകൊണ്ട്
4. രാസോർജ്ജത്തെ വൈദ്യുതോർജ്ജമാക്കി മാറ്റുന്നു.

Activity II

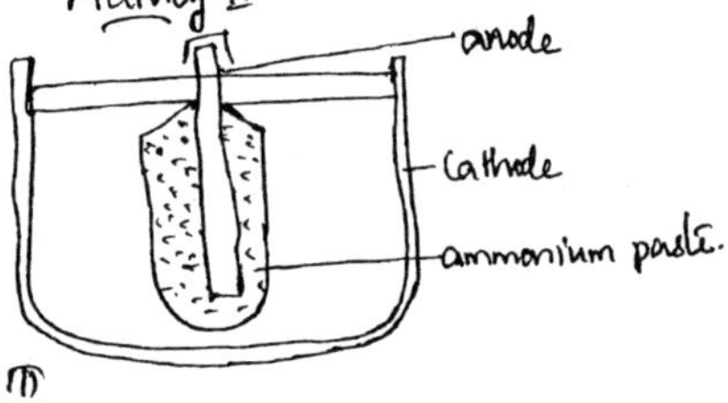

Activity III

1. സെൽ, ബാറ്ററി, [illegible] വയർ, സ്വിച്ച്.
2. ബാറ്ററി വൈദ്യുതി [illegible], വയർ → വൈദ്യുതിയെ ...
3. $C = 6$, $t = 10s$. $I = \frac{10}{6} = 1.6A$

PROBLEM BASED LEARNING

"Problem Based Learning is a strategy for posing significant, contextualized, real world situations and providing resources, guidance and instruction to learners as they develop content knowledge and problem solving skills" (Donnelly, *et al.*, 1993). It is an active process of accessing prior knowledge, making connection between old and new concepts and using the elaboration of relationship to engage in theory construction (Schmdit, 2004).

Problem Based Learning was officially adopted as a Pedagogical approach in 1968 at McMaster University (1974), because the students were unable to apply their substantial amount of basic scientific knowledge and their situations, such as

- Identify the facts on the problem
- Generating their ideas about the problem and identifying just "What is the Problem".
- Finally identifying the things they have to learn about in order to test their hypothesis.

The use of this three step inquiry organizer helps students become familiar with a scientific reasoning process, to fill the gaps in their own knowledge base, and to use their newly acquired knowledge to refine or discard their ideas thus generating a whole new set of learning needs. The aim of Problem Based Learning is to help students to seek out solutions and objectives that can set them on the road to lifelong learning. Problem Based Learning supports and helps effective adult learning and develops better problem solving skills.

Problem Based Learning allows students to learn the fundamental principles of a subject or competency in the content needed to solve a real life situation or problems. Students analyze the problem and look at what they need to do in order to solve the problem at hand effectively and efficiency. It is all about practicing, using and developing processing skills, group skills; critical thinking skills and self directed learning skills, which then leads to problem solving. The success of Problem Based Learning is dependent on the students' ability to combine all of these skills under the guidance of a teacher/ facilitator. This level of engagement in their learning skill will have a profound effect on their external ability to perform and provide a solution to whatever problems they few in the real world.

The core of problem based learning strategy is the use of problems as primary instructional input, leading the learners to improve knowledge and skills. In the Problem Based Learning approach learners work in groups to attain learning objectives. The learning needs of one student complement those of another as the group works together to address all the learning issues. Collaboration within the group is another important element of problem based learning. Problem Based Learning collaboration consists of materials selection, mutual support and co-operation, acknowledgement, continued reinforcement, mutual assistance and assurance in the integration of new information.

Problem based learning is presently used in more than 60 medical schools. It is also used in high schools, middle schools and elementary schools. It offers higher secondary teachers a structured method to help their students build thinking and problem solving skills while students master important subject knowledge.

Methodology of Problem Based Learning

The methodology of problem based learning involves the instructor and students usually in small groups. As the group members' work together to learn and problem solve, they acquire collaborative or team learning skills.

The core of problem based learning strategy is the use of problems as primary instructional inputs, leading the learners to improve knowledge and skills. Collaboration within the group is an important element of problem based learning. Problem based learning consists of four different types of problems.

- *Open ended Problems* with many potential learning issues are very difficult for teachers because they have to help through facilitation process. These are highly challenging for students.
- *Focused Problems* need less facilitation and hence the teacher is mostly free. Learners have clear sense of distinctions in learning.
- *Extended Problem* is the ongoing problem that needs regular facilitation.
- *Culminating Problem* is very interesting to both teachers and learners because it follows a culminating or interesting activity.

The Design of Problem Based Learning can be represented as follows:

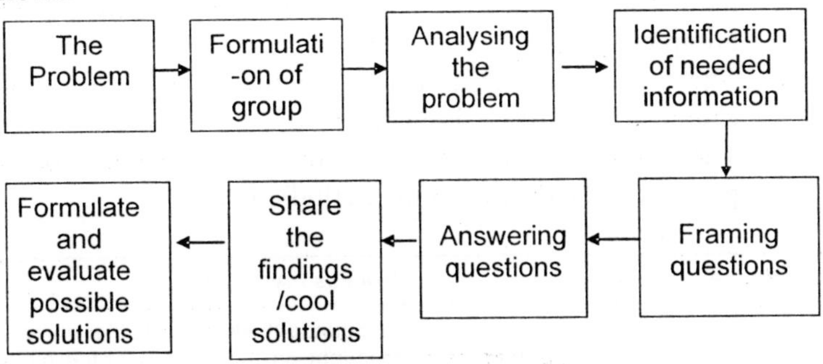

Fig 6.9: Problem based Learning Design

A typical problem based learning session will begin with a group of students; encounter the problem based learning problem scenario. The second stage, the learner make two lists mainly 'facts' and 'need to know'. From the 'need to know' list, the learner has to form learning issues. Learning issues consists of things or information. The activity stage is called the phase of exploration. Then the learner has to list the possible solution. For gathering additional information, the learner has to develop a 'new learning issues' list. It will help the learner to rule in or rule out the possible solution.

LESSON PLAN
USING PROBLEM BASED LEARNING STRATEGY

Name of the Teacher's: Sr. Mary Thomas and Selvi. S
Subject: Chemistry
Name of the School: Govt. HSS Anchal West
Unit: Hydrogen
Standard: XI
Topic: Position of Hydrogen
Duration: 90 minutes

Instructional Objectives

- The pupils identify the problem about the position of Hydrogen.

- The pupils formulate hypothesis and make prediction about the similarities and differences between Hydrogen and other group elements.
- The pupils collect and analyze the information about characteristics of Hydrogen.
- The pupils make inferences and draw conclusions about the position of Hydrogen in the periodic table.

Phase	Process / Activity
Orient students to the problem	Hydrogen is the most abundant element in the universe and the third most abundant on the surface of the globe. Hydrogen has resemblance with both I group elements and VII group elements. But Hydrogen is not included in Ist and XVIIth groups. Teacher asks the students to identify the problem from the situation and asks them to state it. **Consolidation:** • Why Hydrogen has a separate position in the periodic table? • What is the position of Hydrogen in the periodic table?
Organize students for the study	Teacher asks the students to suggest probable reasons of the problem and help them to organize the work in order to solve the problem. **Consolidation:** • Hydrogen has one electron in the outer most shell so it can gain or lose one electron and the size becomes small. Teacher asks the students to prepare a list of the necessary information to be collected for solving the problem. **Consolidation:** • How many protons and electrons are present in Hydrogen? • What is the electronic configuration of Hydrogen atom? • Where is the position of alkali metals in the periodic table? • What is the electronic configuration of halogens? • How many electrons are needed for halogen to obtain the stable state? • How many electrons are needed for hydrogen to obtain the stable state? • What will happen to Hydrogen atom when it loses one electron?

(*Contd.*)

Phase	Process / Activity
	• Are there any similarities between Hydrogen and alkali metals when they lose their electron? • Why halogens and Hydrogen are similar by the gain of one electron in the outer most shell? • What is the reaction of hydrogen with oxides and halides? • Why the reactivity of Hydrogen is lower than that of halogen? • What happens to the size of an atom, if it loses or gains an electron?
Assist independent and group investigation	Teacher divides the students into different small groups and encourages them to gather appropriate information and to search for explanations and solutions. Students discuss these questions in small groups.
Develop and present artifacts and exhibits	Teacher assists students in planning and preparing the result of their investigation about the questions in an appropriate form. Students collect their findings and share their work with others in the whole group. Students write the above questions and the findings of their discussion on the PBL chart. **Consolidation** • Hydrogen has electronic configuration $1s^1$. It contains one electron and one proton. • General electronic configuration of alkali metals is ns^1. Its outer most shell contains only one electron. • Alkali metals are 1 group elements. • Halogens are group 17 elements. They are placed in the right of the periodic table. • Halogens (F, Cl, Br, I, As) has the electronic configuration $ns^2\ np^5$. So they are short by one electron to the corresponding noble gas configuration. • Hydrogen and alkali metals lose or gain their electron in bond formation to form unipositive/uninegative ions. • Hydrogen and halogens are short by one electron to obtain the noble gas electronic configuration. • Like alkali metals, Hydrogen forms their oxides and halides. (eg. HCl, HF) • Hydrogen forms diatomic molecules and large number of covalent compounds like halogens. So it has low reactivity. • Loss of the electron from hydrogen atom decreases its size as compared with normal atomic size.

(*Contd.*)

Phase	Process / Activity
Analysis and evaluate problem solving process.	Students discussed the similarities and differences of hydrogen with alkali metals and halogens and they identified that hydrogen is placed separately in the periodic table because of its unique behaviour. The Teacher asks the students to redefine the problem statement, to go through the problem solving process and find out the steps they adopted for solving the problem.

VII

Testing of Science Process Skills

As teachers, we are greatly interested to know how well our students are doing science or how much they are skilled in science processes. In order to assess this, we must test their performance in authentic contexts and we should see how they feel and value at different situations. The traditional way of testing is focussed only on knowledge domain which is the lowest in Bloom's taxonomy. Enger and Yager (1998) identified six domains of science education. These are:

Nature of Science: What science is, who does it, why it is done, creating context, the big picture

Processes: Mechanisms of science, how research is conducted, Exploring and discovering

Concepts: Content, accumulated science knowledge, knowing and understanding

Applications: uses for and ability to use scientific knowledge, using and applying

Attitudes: Perceptions of science, scientists, science teachers, scientific knowledge, feeling and valuing

Creativity: Thought patterns representing divergence or synergy, imagining and creating

Now the emphasis in teaching has shifted to construction of knowledge based on first hand experiences and therefore the science assessment should not be confined to knowledge alone. It should encompass all the domains of science education. The higher levels of understanding, application, process skills and affective domain are overlooked in assessment. As the emphasis in teaching is shifted to the active process of investigation, the assessment of process skills and scientific inquiry should be integrated into classroom teaching and assessment.

Direct and Indirect Assessment

The traditional paper pencil tests measure learning indirectly. That means, if a particular student is able to answer a prompting question by remembering something taught in the class, it is considered as a clear indication of the student learning. In olden days, this way of assessment was appropriate. But now the importance of recalling information is diminished as it is readily available in World Wide Web. The emphasis in testing is shifted to 'what meaning the students have constructed as a result of instruction and whether they can apply what they have learned.

The paper pencil tests give way to the assessment of student products and performances that yields direct measures of cognitive changes. 'Performance based assessment and performance tests are conducted as hands on science activities representing direct measures of learning, in contrast to multiple choice tests'. The latter gives only indirect indication of learning. But in performance tests, the understanding of a science concept as well as the ability to apply the concept can be assessed. A paper-pencil test will not be fit to measure a student's skill in swimming. A dancer's skill in 'Bharathanatyam' can be measured only through the observation of her stage performance in that particular item.

Such type of performance based assessment is equally suited to science education. Such assessment will help the teacher to know how well the students have met the science lesson objectives. For this, the teacher should put students into such situations where students can create knowledge and apply them. Performance based assessment requires students to involve in active problem soling or interpreting a situation. It is different from merely recalling information or avoiding distracters as in multiple choice items. Some characteristics of performance based tests are the tasks requiring active student involvement and answers are constructed by students.

Techniques for Performance Based Assessment

There are many techniques for assessment which requires students to construct responses to open ended tasks. Some of them like interview and checklists require teacher's to observe or interact with students as and when their data are collected.

Interview

Interview is the face to face method of collecting information. It is a process of communication or interaction where the subject gives the needed information verbally. Interview can be used as a means for assessment before and after instruction. As interview provides one-to-one conversation, and follow up probing we can assess student's personal explanations for natural phenomena. It can be used for identifying their pre and misconceptions. If we interview several students selected randomly from the class, the group patterns of pre and misconceptions can be detected. Here interview is used for diagnostic purpose which helps in instructional planning.

If we use interview after instruction, we can assess the changes occurred in different domains. Areas of continual misunderstanding can also be identified. Teacher can use probing questions for the identification of details of student understanding.

Checklists

Checklists are used for assessing students during individual and group activities. Teacher needs to check whether students follow her directions correctly, making proper measurements, testing predictions by using valid methods or classifying objects properly. Checklists allow the teacher to assess the observable behaviours or exhibited skills which are important for the learning of science. If we use a predesigned checklist, then the task of the teacher is simplified indicating the desired behaviour as present or absent.

The checklists provide an organised way to record student progress in a minimum amount of time. If an additional column is included along with the checklists for adding teacher's comments, its value increases.

i) Sample checklist for assessing science process skills

Component skills	Yes	No	Comments
Observing			
Raising Questions			
Hypothesising			
Predicting			
Finding patterns and relationships			
Communicating effectively			
Defining and making			
Manipulating materials and equipments effectively			
Measuring and calculating			

(ii) Sample checklist for the skill of observation

Process skill	*Component skills*	*Yes*	*No*	*Comments*
Observing	Using the senses to gather information			
	Identifying differences between similar objects or events			
	Identifying similarities between different objects or events			
	Recognising the order in which sequenced events take place			
	Distinguishing from any observations those which are relevant to the problem at hand			

iii) Sample checklist for the skill of raising questions

Process skill	Component skills	Yes	No	Comments
raising questions	Asking questions which lead to inquiry			
	Asking questions based on hypothesis			
	Identifying questions which they can answer by their own investigations			
	Putting questions into a form, which indicates the investigation which are to be carried out			
	Recognising that some questions cannot be answered by inquiry			

iv) Sample checklist for the skill of Hypothesising

Process skill	Component skills	Yes	No	Comments
Hypothesising	Attempting to explain observations or relationships in terms of some principle or concept			
	Applying concepts or knowledge gained in some situation to help under-standing or solving a problem in another			
	Recognising that there can be more than one possible explanation of an event			
	Recognising the need to test explanation by gathering more evidence			
	Suggesting explanations which are testable, even if unlikely			

v) Sample checklist for the skill of Predicting

Process skill	Component skills	Yes	No	Comments
Predicting	Making use of evidence to make a prediction			
	Explicitly use patterns or relationship to make a prediction			
	Justifying how a prediction was made in terms of present evidence or past experience			
	Showing caution in making assumptions about the general application of a pattern beyond available evidence			
	Making use of patterns to extrapolate to cases where no information has been gathered			

Science Journals

Science journals can provide evidence for student progress in multiple domains. It may be used for collecting data during an investigation, recording the activities done during a project work, or to summarise the learning for the day. Then that particular work can be utilised for assessing skill development. Journal works can be utilised for assessing students' ability to apply what they learned in classroom to their lives outside the school, if they are asked to make entries in such a way.

Assessment of students' journal is mainly depending dependent on the objectives of learning. If the purpose of the journal is to collect and record data from an experiment, the teacher has to check the accuracy and organisation of the data. Students can record the whole discovery or inquiry activities done by them, including details of their observation, questions arise in their minds, the possible suggestions came to their minds, and the alternate designs for testing the hypotheses. Apart these, journal entries can also be used asused as an excellent source of assessment data regarding the affective outcomes related to learning.

Inquiry Reports

Inquiry reports are the documentation of procedures and results of students' investigations. An inquiry may start from teacher's question or from students' own inquisitiveness. For example, students are learning about universe. Some of the students are contented with what they learned learnt in the classroom. Others may want to know more. One student may be interested in knowing more about thermo nuclear reactions in stars. Another student may be interested in the death of stars. Each one's area of interest may be different. They may be asked to formulate a question that may serve as a focus of their inquiry. Each student or group will collect data pertaining to their study from multifaceted resources ranging from internet to observation.

After collecting the information, each student may be called to share on their information before the whole class. This can be done either informally as in a science talk or as a formal presentation by using posters or power point presentations. It may be an oral presentation supported by written materials and audiovisual aids.

Though inquiry reports provide evidence of student performance, it places some critical challenges for assessment. It is difficult to assess the original interest and inquisitiveness and initiative from students' part. When we come to the problem of assessing the amount of information gained through the inquiry, the student is the best person than the teacher to assess it. By assessing such inquiry process by the student, he may get more insight into his own knowledge and thinking process. This will lead to reflection on gaining of knowledge and skill through inquiry.

Rating Scale on Reflection on Learning through Inquiry Reports

Name of the Student: .... *Subject*: ....
Standard: .... *Division*: ....
Title of the Inquiry Project: .... *Roll Number*: ....

Instruction: Put a tick mark on the number that best reflects your learning.

Sl. No.	Statements	Ratings				
		1	2	3	4	5
01	I got a clear understanding of the topic by conducting the inquiry.					
02	I used all possible sources of information for accomplishing the project.					
03	I learn how to draw inference from the data pertaining to the inquiry project.					
04	I can formulate hypothesis with more confidence than I did before starting the project.					
05	I can explain with authenticity what I have learned to somebody else.					
06	By conducting the inquiry my interest in the topic has increased.					

Investigation Reports

Investigation reports and inquiry reports are similar in some respects. The student is preparing the report after making an investigation. It is different from inquiry reports in a way that the investigative technique should follow some particular structure. Reporting investigation helps the students to organise their thought process. This will create subtle differences in their observations and conclusions. The structure of investigation reports should include hypothesis formulation and testing in a trial and error basis, documenting, collecting and organizing data, generating models, experimenting, reflecting and inventing.

Guidelines to the investigation reports vary according to the form of investigation. All investigation reports should have some common elements.

- A problem to be investigated
- Description of the steps to be followed in the investigation
- Organisation and summary of collected data
- Details of drawing inference.

Quality of the report depends on students' level of understanding, ability, experience and interest in conducting investigation. Each student will get a personal experience with the investigatory activities in terms of questions, data collection, hypothesizing and drawing inference. This investigatory activity will develop the skill and confidence in students to solve real problems. Therefore during evaluation process, rather than product, this should find more emphasis.

Test of Process Outcomes in Physics

Test of Process Outcomes in Physics is a standardized tool for assessing science process skills in Physics developed by the authors. The details of the skills and sub skills used for the test are given below.

1. *Recognising and Defining a Problem*: Pupils recognise specific problem in a new situation, Pupils isolate the single idea of a major problem, Pupils state problem as definite and concise questions
2. *Formulating Hypotheses*: Pupils suggest tentative solutions to the problem
3. *Collecting Data:* Pupils select suitable test of the hypothesis, Pupils select suitable variables to be included in the experiment, Pupils selects the controlling variables, Pupil

observes objects and phenomena, Pupil measure objects and changes, Pupil selects equipments for experiments

4. *Interpreting Data:* Pupils organise data collected, Pupils identify relationships, Pupils interpret relationship
5. *Evaluating Hypothesis:* Pupils formulate conclusions on the basis of relationship found, Pupils relate hypothesis in relation to the data interpreted
6. *Pupils Formulate Generalisations*: Pupils apply conclusions to new situations, Pupils formulate generalisations on the basis of relationship identified and conclusions formed and applied

Preparation of Items

Since the purpose of the test was to measure Process outcomes in Physics of the secondary school students in Kerala, the items prepared were from the area of secondary school Physics. The authors took precautions to include items which have practical applications in day-to-day life. Special care was given so that the mental operations while answering the questions were the natural outcome of science teaching and learning in classroom situations. The following books and other forms of literature were freely used as guidelines for preparing the test items:

Science teaching and testing (Nedelsky, 1965).
Handbook for formative and summative evaluation of student learning (Bloom, *et al.*, 1971)
Science education in nineteen countries: An empirical study (Comber and Keeves, 1973).
Integrated process skill test (Okey and Dillashow, 1979)
Middle grade integrated process skill test (Padilla and Cronin, 1978)
Test of Process outcomes in biology (Suresh, 1991)

The Test of Process Outcomes in Physics includes six subtests. Each subtest measures the acquisition of each major skill given in the above list. Each subtest contains ten items of objective multiple choice type. For each item, four alternative responses are given. The respondent has to select the correct alternative. The choice of correct alternative by the respondent would indicate that he/she has achieved the outcome in question. The explanation given below regarding each skill served as guidelines for the preparation of the items.

1. *Recognising and Defining Problem:* The test items under this head present problematic situations before the respondent. The respondent has to identify the problem area, isolate the single major idea of the problem, and has to define the problem using correct language.
2. *Formulating Hypotheses:* In this subtest the subject is presented stated problems. He has to suggest suitable solutions to the problem in hand, based on the conditions presented in the items. The hypothesis should direct one to further investigation. Four alternative hypotheses were given along with each test item. The task of the subject is to decide which hypothesis is the most suitable and reasonable one.
3. *Collecting Data:* In this subtest, students are given actual learning situations for particular problems. The tasks of the students are to identify the manipulated variables, the dependent variables and controlled variables in the problem situations and to describe how the variables are controlled. The correct response to items under this category would indicate that the student has attained the outcome in question.
4. *Interpreting Data:* Here the tasks assigned to the respondent are to describe the collected data in verbal or nonverbal form, organise the data so as to facilitate effective communication, to draw inference based up on the collected data and to construct tables.
5. *Evaluation of Hypotheses:* In this subtest the problem stated and the hypotheses formulated are presented to the subject. He has to design an investigation for testing the hypothesis, to select suitable test from the alternate tests given and to evaluate the hypotheses on the basis of the given data. The student has to see whether the evidence is consistent with the logical requirements of the hypotheses.
6. *Formulating Generalisations:* Here the tasks given to the

respondent are to apply the conclusions to new situations and formulate generalisations on the basis of relationships identified. Twenty items each were pooled initially for each subtest. Some of the test items were adapted from school Physics and from available literature cited earlier. A panel of Physics teachers were formed for establishing the face validity. Each item was discussed at length in terms of its appropriateness, complexity, subject matter and exactness of information. Based on the scrutiny of experts, fifteen items were selected for each subtest which was found appropriate and valid. These subtests constitute the draft TPOP. Instructions for the respondents, scoring key and appropriate response sheet were prepared.

The draft test of Process Outcomes in Physics was pre-tried out to a group of ten students of ninth standard to ensure clarity of wordings and directions. Based on the pre-try out final draft test of Process Outcomes in Physics consisting of ninety items, fifteen items for each subtest was prepared and got printed.

Standardisation of TPOP

The draft test was administered to a representative sample of 400 students drawn from standard nine of the secondary schools of Kottayam, Kannur and Malappuram districts. One score was given to the correct response of each test item. The sum of the scores for the ninety items was taken as the total score of the test. From among the responses 370 response sheets which were complete in every respect were selected for the psychometric procedures of item analysis.

The 370 answer scripts were arranged in the descending order of the total score. The highest 27 per cent and the lowest 27 per cent with respect to the total scores were separated. There were 100 response sheets each from upper and lower levels.

Each response sheet in the upper and lower levels were examined. The number of response sheets in the upper and lower groups who answered each item correctly was found out. The indices of item discrimination and difficulty were estimated by using the procedure suggested by Ebel (1965).

The difficulty level and discriminating power of each item were estimated by using the following formulae

Index of item difficulty Dv = (U+L)/2N *100
Index of item discrimination Di = (U-L)/N

Where 'U' = the number of correct responses for any item n the upper group
'L' = the umber of correct responses for any item n the lower group
'2N' = total number of answer scripts in the upper and lower levels
'N' = 100 since the upper and lower groups stands for 27 per cent of the total group of 370 which is equal to 100 for both upper and lower groups.

On the basis of the indices of difficulty and discrimination, items were rated. Items with difficulty index between 65 and 35 (on the assumption that the items of difficulty level of 50 have the highest discriminating power) were identified. From among these items, items with highest discriminating power were selected. Only items of discriminating power of .30 and above were selected for the final test. Thus ten items from each subtest were selected and they were arranged n the increasing order of difficulty. The final test of Process Outcomes in Physics includes a covering page with specific directions for the guidance of the students and six subtests containing ten items each.

Validity and Reliability of Test of Process Outcomes in Physics

Content validity of test of Process Outcomes in Physics which requires the determination of the adequacy of each item to be a sample of the process skills which are supposed to be measured, was ensured through careful planning of the test, satisfying the adequacy of planning of test items by following the standard theoretical models of the construct to be measured and meticulous analysis of the testitems by experts. In the final TPOP all the six subtests were given equal weightage by including equal number of items in each.

The Item Analysis Data for the Test of Process Outcomes in Physics

Test I

S. No.	*U*	*L*	*Difficulty Value* $Dv = \frac{U+L}{N} \times 100$	*Discrimination* $\frac{U-L}{N}$	*R*	*A*	*S.A.*
1.	68	35	51.5	0.33	-	A	6
2.	35	46	40.5	-0.11	R	-	-
3.	57	15	36.0	0.42	-	A	9
4.	85	43	64.0	0.42	-	A	1
5.	91	63	76.0	0.29	R	-	-
6.	85	65	75.0	0.20	R	-	-
7.	85	27	56.0	0.58	-	A	5
8.	67	33	50.0	0.34	-	A	7
9.	47	25	36.0	0.22	R	-	-
10.	81	37	59.0	0.34	-	A	3
11.	50	47	43.5	0.03	R	-	-
12.	73	41	57.0	0.32	-	A	4
13.	66	33	49.5	0.33	-	A	8
14.	86	42	64.0	0.44	-	A	2
15.	56	14	35.0	0.42	-	A	10

Test II

S. No.	*U*	*L*	*Difficulty Value* $Dv = \frac{U+L}{N} \times 100$	*Discrimination* $\frac{U-L}{N}$	*R*	*A*	*S.A.*
1.	87	46	66.5	0.41	-	A	2
2.	54	22	38.0	0.32	-	A	8
3.	56	32	44.0	0.24	R	-	-
4.	71	25	48.0	0.46	-	A	6
5.	56	25	40.0	0.31	-	A	7
6.	71	37	54.0	0.34	-	A	4
7.	60	12	36.0	0.48	-	A	10
8.	75	33	54.0	0.42	-	A	3
9.	78	24	51.0	0.54	-	A	5

10.	94	42	68.0	0.52	-	A	1
11.	34	14	24.0	0.20	R	-	-
12.	52	24	38.0	0.28	-	A	9
13.	42	21	31.0	0.21	R	-	-
14.	49	27	38.0	0.22	R	-	-
15.	56	36	46.0	0.20	R	-	-

Test III

S. No.	*U*	*L*	*Difficulty Value* $Dv = \frac{U+L}{N} \times 100$	*Discrimination* $\frac{U-L}{N}$	*R*	*A*	*S.A.*
1.	19	6	12.5	0.13	R	-	-
2.	38	25	31.5	0.13	R	-	-
3.	46	24	35.0	0.22	R	-	-
4.	59	21	40.0	0.38	-	A	10
5.	64	21	42.5	0.43	-	A	4
6.	60	24	42.0	0.36	-	A	6
7.	58	26	42.0	0.31	-	A	7
8.	56	26	41.0	0.30	-	A	8
9.	66	24	45.0	0.42	-	A	2
10.	60	20	40.0	0.40	-	A	9
11.	69	24	46.5	0.45	-	A	1
12.	58	28	43.0	0.30	-	A	3
13.	37	16	26.5	0.21	R	-	-
14.	39	24	31.5	0.15	R	-	-
15.	62	22	42.0	0.40	-	A	5

Test IV

S. No.	*U*	*L*	*Difficulty Value* $Dv = \frac{U+L}{N} \times 100$	*Discrimination* $\frac{U-L}{N}$	*R*	*A*	*S.A.*
1.	66	24	45.0	0.42	-	A	6
2.	58	26	42.0	0.32	-	A	7
3.	30	32	31.0	-0.02	R	-	-
4.	79	38	58.5	0.41	-	A	3
5.	44	32	38.0	0.12	R	-	-

6.	80	37	58.5	0.43	-	A	2
7.	51	20	35.5	0.31	-	A	9
8.	87	28	57.5	0.59	-	A	1
9.	56	16	36.0	0.40	-	A	8
10.	49	39	34.0	0.10	R	-	-
11.	32	29	30.5	0.03	R	-	-
12.	69	30	49.5	0.39	-	A	4
13.	62	29	49.5	0.33	-	A	5
14.	36	32	34.0	0.04	R	-	-
15.	53	16	34.5	0.37	-	A	10

Test V

S. No.	*U*	*L*	*Difficulty Value* $Dv = \frac{U+L}{N} \times 100$	*Discrimination* $\frac{U-L}{N}$	*R*	*A*	*S.A.*
1.	65	21	43.0	0.44	-	A	2
2.	48	15	29.0	0.33	-	A	9
3.	66	23	44.5	0.43	-	A	1
4.	33	17	25.0	0.16	R	-	-
5.	52	22	37.0	0.30	-	A	6
6.	29	13	22.0	0.16	R	-	-
7.	43	15	29.0	0.28	-	A	10
8.	28	19	23.5	0.09	R	-	-
9.	34	15	24.5	0.19	R	-	-
10.	58	22	40.0	0.36	-	A	4
11.	53	20	36.5	0.33	-	A	7
12.	40	23	31.5	0.17	R	-	-
13.	61	22	41.5	0.39	-	A	3
14.	55	25	40.0	0.30	-	A	5
15.	52	19	35.5	0.33	-	A	8

Test VI

S. No.	*U*	*L*	*Difficulty Value* $Dv = \frac{U+L}{N} \times 100$	*Discrimination* $\frac{U-L}{N}$	*R*	*A*	*S.A.*
1.	47	15	31.0	0.32	-	A	10
2.	37	18	27.5	0.19	R	-	-
3.	70	30	50.0	0.40	-	A	4

4.	60	25	42.5	0.35	-	A	8
5.	61	30	45.5	0.31	-	A	7
6.	74	32	53.0	0.42	-	A	3
7.	59	26	42.5	0.33	-	A	9
8.	72	26	49.0	0.46	-	A	5
9.	66	25	45.5	0.41	-	A	6
10.	75	35	55.0	0.40	-	A	2
11.	32	16	24.0	0.16	R	-	-
12.	48	25	36.5	0.23	R	-	-
13.	42	22	32.0	0.20	R	-	-
14.	78	33	55.5	0.45	-	A	1
15.	46	20	33.0	0.26	R	-	-

The construct validity of the test was estimated by using average marks obtained in Physics for the first and second terminal examinations of standard nine pupils treated as the external criteria. The average marks in Physics of 100 pupils of standard nine were used for this purpose. The scores obtained in the TPOP were correlated with the average Physics scores. The coefficient of correlation was found to be 0.77.

The split-half reliability was estimated for the whole test as well as for the component test. The coefficients of correlations corrected for shortening using Spearman Brown formula are presented in Table 4.3.

Table 4.3: Reliability Coefficients Corrected by Using Spearman Brown Formula

Tests	Reliability Coefficient
Subtest I	.92
Subtest II	.94
Subtest III	.78
Subtest IV	.89
Subtest V	.92
Subtest VI	.92
Whole test	.96

Reliability using Kuder Richardson formula was estimated. The reliability by using this method (for N=100) was found to be 0.96. The validity and reliability coefficients reported here show that TPOP is a reasonably valid and reliable tool for measuring process outcomes in Physics.

Test of Process Outcomes in Physics

Instructions

In this test, there are six subtests. For each item in this test, four answers 'a', 'b', 'c', and 'd' are given. Out of which only one answer is correct. Answers should mark on the response sheet separately given to you.

In the response sheet, letters 'a', 'b', 'c' and 'd' are marked against each option. Find the correct answer and mark 'x' in the column below the correct answer.

If the answer marked by you is found to be wrong, draw a square □ around it and mark 'x' in the proper place.

When the investigator says 'start', start answering the test and when he says 'stop', stop answering. After the test, response sheet and test booklet are to be returned to the invigilator.

If you have any doubt regarding answering the test the invigilator will help you in giving necessary clarifications.

e.g. A cosmonaut who is far away from the earth experiences darkness around him. The most suitable reason for this is:

a. There is no chance for the reflection of light since the space is vacuum.
b. Space absorbs light rays
c. The cosmonaut is far away from the sun.
d. There is no source of light in the space.

Answer:

a	b	c	d
×			

Test I

1. When a small glass sphere and a stone are rolled in a smooth surface the stone stop abruptly after moving a short distance while the glass sphere covers a longer distance.
   Here the problem is...
   a. Whether the glass sphere is lighter than the stone?

b. Whether the surface area of the glass sphere is greater than that of the stone?
c. To what extent the smooth surface of the glass sphere influences the friction when compared to the influence of the rough surface of the stone?
d. How does the density of the stone differ from that of glass sphere?

2 The weight of a stone immersed in water is found to be lesser than its actual weight when it is measured using a spring balance. Here the problem is ...
a. Does the spring balance show lesser weight for the object than its actual weight?
b. Does water exerts an upward force on a body which is immersed in it?
c. Whether the parts of the stone in touch with water get dissolved in it?
d. Whether there was any possibility for the overflow of water when stone was immersed in it?

2. When telegraph wires are laid, sufficient sag is given. The problem here is...
a. Whether the loose wires have more capacity for propagation?
b. Which metal is used for making the telegraph wires?
c. How thermal conductivity and electrical conductivity of the metal wires are related?
d. How does the difference in atmospheric temperature affect telegraph wires?

4. Sound is not heard when an electric bell is operated inside an evacuated bell jar. The problem here is...
a. Why did an evacuated bell jar use for the experiment?
b How does the presence of air influence the working of the bell?
c. How does the electric operate in the absence of air?
d. Does sound need a medium for its propagation?

5. When a compound bar of steel and copper is heated, the bar bends with copper outside. The problem here is...
a. How much the temperature of the compound bar rises when it is heated?

b. Whether the proportion of steel and copper used in the construction of the compound bar affects bending?
c. How does the rate of expansion of steel and copper differ?
d. How do the heat resistant powers of steel and copper differ?

6. A person cannot see anything clearly for sometime, when he enters a dark room from bright light. Here the problem is...
   a. How does the bright light affect sight?
   b. How does the bright light affect iris?
   c. How does the iris respond to the changes in the brightness of light?
   d. How does the brightness of the light influence the deficiencies of the eye?
7. Mountaineers suffer from nose bleeding at high altitudes. The problem here is...
   a. How do the changes in the atmospheric pressure at high altitudes affect living things?
   b. How does the weather at high altitudes affect living things?
   c. How is atmospheric temperature at high altitude different from that at sea level?
   d. How is humidity at higher altitude different from that at sea level?
8. Reservoirs in hydro-electric power stations are built in high places. The problem here is...
   a. What is the function of reservoirs in hydro-electric power stations?
   b. How far the height of water flow is related to the quantity of electricity produced?
   c. How far the capacity of reservoirs is related to the quantity of electricity produced?
   d. What are the factors which influence the quantity of electricity produced?
9. A coin placed at the bottom of a trough filled with water seems to be raised from its actual position. The problem here is...
   a. What is the nature of the image formed when rays from the coin falls on the eye-lens?

b. How does the depth of the water in the trough affect the formation of image?
c. To what height the coin appears to be raised when it is observed from above?
d. How do the optical densities of water and air influence the position of the image?

10. A tin-can filled with steam become mis-shaped on cooling. The problem here is...
    a. How does the temperature of tin-can influence its shape?
    b. Whether the change in pressure inside the tin-can on the liquidification of steam is lesser than atmospheric pressure?
    c. Ho does the atmospheric temperature influence the shape of tin-can?
    d. How much pressure is exerted by steam on tin-can?

Test II

1. When rails are laid, a small gap is left between consecutive rails. What is the most suitable reason for this?
   a. The possibility of expansion of rails with the increase in atmospheric temperature
   b. The possibility of expansion of rails due to the pressure
   c. To resist the great speed of the train
   d. To aid the acceleration of the train
2. An athlete runs a little distance before a long jump. Suggest the reason for this?
   a. In order to utilize the inertia of rest gained through running
   b. In order to utilize the inertia of motion gained through running
   c. In order to increase his confidence through running
   d. In order to stimulate his muscles through running
3. Even though, gases have freedom to move, air remains in the earth's atmosphere. Suggest the most suitable reason for this?
   a. Gases are not attracted towards space.
   b. Atmospheric gases repel each other.
   c. Atmospheric gases attract each other
   d. Earth attracts gases.

4. A green leaf appears to be dark in red light. What is the most suitable reason for this?
   a. All substances appear to be dark in red light.
   b. The leaf absorbs red light and does not reflect other colours.
   c. the leaf absorbs and reflects red light.
   d. Red light is so feeble that the leaf cannot be seen.
5. When an inflated balloon placed on the smooth surface of a table, was pricked with a pin, air gushed out and the balloon moved in the opposite direction. The most suitable reason for this may be...
   a. The air gushed out through the hole with a high velocity.
   b. the weight of the balloon decreased and the movement became easy.
   c. The smooth surface of the table made the balloon friction free.
   d. The air gushing out exerted force on the balloon in the opposite direction.
6. When we tread on mud, our legs get immersed in it. But when we stand on wooden plank over it the plank does not get immersed. The reason for this may be
   a. When we stand on the wooden plank the exerted on the mud is less.
   b. Since the area of the wooden plank is greater than that of the feet, the pressure exerted on the mud is more.
   c. Since Atmospheric gases repel each other e the area of the wooden plank is greater than that of the feet, the pressure exerted on the mud is less.
   d. When we tread on the plank, the force exerted on the mud is more.
7. When a peacock feather is rubbed in between the pages of a book, it spreads like a fan. The most suitable reason for this may be...
   a. Static electricity is induced in the feather since the humidity is vapourised by the heat produced in the feather.
   b. With the rise in temperature the humidity in the feather vapourises and thereby its volume increases.

  c. The static electricity induced among the hairs of the feather has the same charge and they repel.
  d. The static electricity induced among the hairs of the feather has the opposite charge and they repel.

8. If a card board boat with a piece of soap at its hind end, is placed on water it moves in random direction. The most suitable reason for this may be...
   a. Surface tension decreases when card board decreases in water.
   b. Surface tension increases when card board decreases in water.
   c. Surface tension of water near the boat increases when soap dissolves in water.
   d. Surface tension of water near the boat decreases when soap dissolves in water.
9. More force is needed to drink through a straw at high altitudes. The reason for this may be...
   a. It is difficult to suck the drink, because it is too cold
   b. It is difficult to suck the drink, because it is too hot.
   c. Since the atmospheric pressure is low, the liquid exerts only a slight force in order to fill the straw.
   d. The high amount of atmospheric pressure can exert less force, which is not enough to fill the straw with drink.
10. People like to wear light coloured dresses in summer. The reason for this may be...
    a. Light coloured dresses reflect more heat.
    b. Light coloured dresses absorb more heat than others
    c. More heat penetrates through light coloured dresses.
    d. Light coloured dresses absorb humidity.

Test III

1. A group of students decided to experiment on and study "capillary rise" by using glass tubes. Which of the following factors can they vary during the experiments?
   1. Radius of the tubes
   2. Shapes of the tubes
   3. Nature of the liquid

4. Shape of the container of the liquid
    a. 1, 2
    b. 1, 3
    c. 1, 4
    d. 2, 4

2. You are given a cylindrical tin vessel and nail in order to prove that liquid pressure operates equally towards all directions. In this experiment which factor will you keep constant?
    a. Direction of the stream
    b. The size of the tin can
    c. The height of the holes
    d. the distance at which the stream falls on the floor

3. Sheela assumes that the rate of vapourisation depends on the nature of the liquid. Which of the following factors are to be observed by her in order to test her assumption?
    1. Density of the liquids
    2. Volume of the container
    3. Rate of vapourisation
    4. Temperature
    5. Pressure
        a. 1, 2, 3, 4, 5
        b. 1, 2, 3, 4
        c. 1, 2, 3, 5
        d. 1, 3, 4, 5

4. A group of pupils were studying the time taken by bodies of light weight and heavy weight to reach the ground from a height. Which of the factors given below influence the time of fall?
    a. Presence of air
    b. Weight of the body
    c. Height from which the body falls
    d. Weather

5. Some pupils were studying the power felt on different parts of a bar magnet. They observed the number of pins attracted at different parts of the magnet. Which of the following information is to be included among the data collected?
    a. The distance of each point in the magnet from the centre and the number of pins that each point can attract.

b. Shape of the magnet and the number of pins that can be attracted by them
c. The weight of each magnet and the number of pins that can be attracted by them
d. The distance to a point outside the magnet from the magnetic centre and the number of pins that can be attracted at that point.

Questions 6 to 8 are based on the Situations Given Below:

Bobby and his friends were placing ice cubes in water and measuring their heights above the surface level of water.

6. In this experiment, which of the factors given below has to be changed?
   a. Height of the ice cubes
   b. Volume of the ice cubes
   c. Temperature of water
   d. Surface area of water
7. Which of the following factors should be kept constant, in this experiment?
   a. Height of the ice cubes
   b. Volume of the ice cubes
   c. Temperature of water
   d. Surface area of water
8. Which of the following factors is subjected to change because of the changes in the height of the ice cubes?
   a. Height of the ice cubes above the surface of the water
   b. Temperature of water
   c. Density of water
   d. Surface area of water
9. Suppose you desire to prove Archimedes principle. You are given a spring balance, a body, and a filled overflow bottle. Which of the following observations will you record in your note book?
   1. Loss of weight of the body in liquid
   2. Weight of the out flowing liquid
   3. Volume of the out flowing liquid
   4. Volume of the liquid that can be filled in the container
      a. 1, 2
      b. 2, 4

c. 3, 4
d. 2, 4

10. Which of the following factors can be overlooked in a study of strength of magnet?
    a. Size of the magnet
    b. Material of the magnet
    c. Number of lines of flux
    d. The attractive force exerted on magnet by magnetic substances

Test IV

1. When a flask is heated gradually after fitting a balloon tightly over its mouth, the balloon gets inflated. From this it can be inferred that...
    a. The air inside the flask expanded when it is heated
    b. The flask and the balloon are arranged airtight
    c. The volume of flask decreases when heated
    d. There are small drops of water in the flask.
2. It is difficult to pull out the cap of a pen with an oily hand. The inference which can be drawn from this is...
    a. Oil helps decrease the friction between the hand and the cap of the pen
    b. Oil helps increase the friction between the hand and the cap of the pen
    c. Tightly fitted cap becomes loose in the presence of oil
    d. Oil facilitates the movement of the hand
3. Beena was pouring a cold drink in to a tumbler. After a second, drops of water appeared on the outer side of the tumbler. From this it can be inferred that...
    a. The drops of water has come from the drink inside
    b. Water drops have leaked out
    c. Water drops were formed by the liquidification of vapour in the surroundings.
    d. If the temperature of the atmosphere is higher, there will be more drops of water.

Questions 4 and 5 are based on the situation given below:

Sheela was checking the accuracy of the inference that rate of evaporation depends upon the temperature of the liquid. It was found that when the temperature of the liquid was 40°C, the rate of evaporation was 0.1 ml/s and at 50°C, the rate of evaporation was 0.2 ml/s, at 70°C, it was 0.4ml/s and at 80°C, it was 0.55ml/s.

4. Which of the tables given below present the data in most conducive manner to draw the inference?

a.

Temperature (°C)	Rate of evaporation (ml/s)
40	0.1
50	0.2
60	0.25
70	0.4
80	0.55

b.

Temperature (°C)	Rate of evaporation (ml/s)
40	0.1
50	0.2
80	0.55
70	0.4
60	0.25

c.

Temperature (°C)	Rate of evaporation (ml/s)
70	0.4
80	0.55
60	0.25
50	0.2
40	0.1

d.

Temperature (°C)	Rate of evaporation (ml/s)
60	0.25
50	0.2
40	0.1
80	0.55
70	0.4

5. What do you infer from the data given above?
   a. As temperature increases, rate of evaporation decreases
   b. As temperature increases, rate of evaporation increases
   c. Rate of evaporation is unaffected by the temperature of the liquid
   d. Rate of evaporation depends upon the nature of the liquid

6. Mohan found that the level of water inside a tumbler is same before and after dissolving sugar (a tea spoonful) in it. The inference which can be drawn from this is....
   a. Water is a good solvent.
   b. Sugar reacts with water
   c. The tumbler is expanded due to heat produced during the dissolving of sugar.
   d. The sugar molecules were accommodated within the vacant spaces in water molecules
7. Even though atmosphere exerts force downwards, we do not experience it. It can be inferred from this that....
   a. Atmospheric pressure is exerted on our body in equal quantity from all sides.
   b. The pressure with in our body is greater than that the atmospheric pressure.
   c. Atmospheric pressure does not influence human beings
   d. The pressure of the atmosphere is so low that it can be neglected.
8. Students in a class were studying the velocity of sound. They recorded the time taken to hear the sound produced by striking together two wooden strips at different distance from the observer. When the distances were 320m, 160m,640m and 960m, the time taken to hear the sound were 1s, 0.5s, 2s and 3s respectively. How will you arrange this data in such a way that the result is communicated most clearly?

a.

distance (m)	time taken to hear the sound (s)
160	0.5
320	1
640	2
960	3

b.

distance (m)	time taken to hear the sound (s)
960	3
640	2
320	1
160	
0.5	

c.

distance (m)	time taken to hear the sound (s)
320	1
160	0.5
960	3
640	2

d.

distance (m)	time taken to hear the sound (s)
640	2
960	3
160	0.5
320	1

9. Sheena filled half of a bottle with water using a funnel. While filling the remaining space in the bottle, she raised the funnel a little and then the speed of water falling to the bottle increased. The inference which can be drawn from this is.....
   a. Bottle was filled with air
   b. The air in the bottle went out when the funnel was raised
   c. The speed of outgoing air and speed of incoming water are equal.
   d. The mouth of the bottle and the end of the funnel was filled with water.
10. Students in a science class were studying the change in liquid pressure with the change in depth. On a tin can of 30 cms height, five identical holes were made, which were of 5 cms, 10 cms, 15 cms, 20 cms and 25 cms heights from the base of the can. When the can was filled with water it gushed out through each pore and hit the ground at distances 18 cms, 15 cms, 12 cms, 9 cms and 6 cms respectively. From this it can be inferred that......

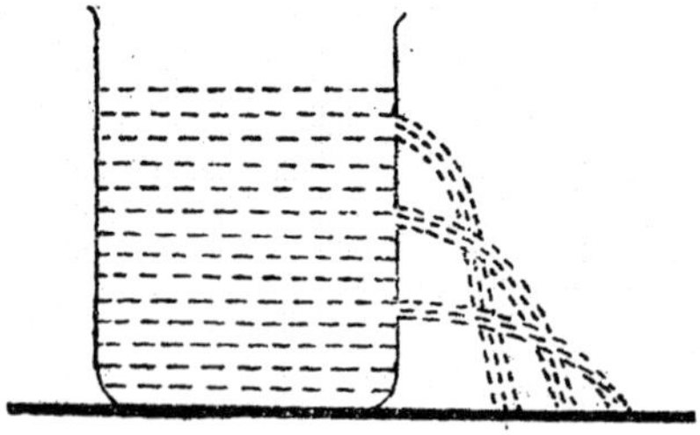

   a. Liquid pressure increases as depth of the liquid increases
   b. Liquid pressure decreases as depth of the liquid increases

c. There is no relationship between height of the liquid column and liquid pressure.
d. Liquid pressure changes according to the nature of the liquid

Test V

1. Which of the following is the most suitable test to prove the assumption that the time taken to melt ice in atmosphere depends on the atmospheric temperature?
   a. Keep ice cubes of same volume in open atmosphere and observe the time taken by each ice cube to melt.
   b. Take two ice cubes of the same volume and keep one in open atmosphere and the other in a room where a fridge is kept. Observe the time taken by each to melt.
   c. Take ice cubes of different volumes. Keep them in a room, where a fridge is kept. Observe the time taken by each to melt.
   d. Keep ice cubes of different volumes in open atmosphere and observe the time taken by them to melt.
2. Which of the following experiment is best to prove that resistance of air is the reason for a heavy body reaches the ground before a light body, even though they are dropped from the same height?
   a. Place a coin and a feather inside a glass tube and close it. Invert the tube suddenly. Measure the time taken by the coin and by the feather to reach the bottom.
   b. Place a coin and a feather inside an evacuated glass tube and invert it suddenly. Count the time taken by each to reach the bottom.
   c. Take a coin inside a glass tube and a feather in another similar glass tube. Close the tubes and invert them suddenly. Count he time taken by the coin and the feather to reach the bottom.
   d. Place five coins and five feathers inside a glass tube. Close the tube and invert it suddenly. Observe the time taken by each to reach the bottom.
3. Select the simplest experiment to prove that the rate of expansion is different for different liquids.
   a. Take three similar boiling tubes and pour alcohol in the

first tube, glycerine in the second, and water in the third tube. Heat them in a water bath. Observe the rise in liquid levels.

b. Take three boiling tubes of different sizes and pour alcohol in the first, glycerine in the second and water in the third tube. Heat them in a water bath. Observe the rise in liquid levels.

c. Take three boiling tubes of same size and fill the first with kerosene, second with alcohol and third with glycerine. Heat them so as to reach at different temperatures. Observe the rise in liquid levels.

d. Take three boiling tubes of different sizes. Fill them with kerosene, alcohol and glycerine and heat them so as to reach at different temperatures. Cool them and observe the liquid levels after fifteen minutes.

4. Which of the following experiment is most suitable to test the inference that surface tension is related to surface area.

   a. Make frames of different sizes and shapes by using iron wire. Tie thread on these. Dip the frames in soap water and note how long the soap films remain in the frames.

   b. Make frames of different sizes by using iron wire and tie thread on it. Dip them in soap solution and observe how long the soap films remain on the thread.

   c. Make frames of different shapes with different metals. Attach thread on them and dip them in soap solution.

   d. Attach thread s to metal frames of different shapes and dip them in different types of liquids.

5. Sheela got two lenses—one convex and one concave—on a cloudy day. Which test you will recommend for her to distinguish between them?

   a. Move the lens to the left while observing the image of a nearby object.

   b. Focus sunlight on a paper using each lens.

   c. Observe the nature of the image of an object which is far from the lens.

   d. Observe the nature of the image of an object which is near to the lens.

6. Neena wants to test the statement, 'liquid pressure exerts in all directions equally'. Which test would you suggest for her?
   a. Make holes using a nail at same height from the base on a cylindrical tin can. Fill the tin can with water. Compare the distance at which the streams of water coming out of the can hit the ground.
   b. Make some holes in a tin can here and there. Fill the tin can with water. Compare the distances from the can to the falling place of water streams.
   c. Make holes at different height from the base of the can. Fill it with water and compare the distances at which the streams of water fall on the ground.
   d. Take two tin cans of different heights. Make holes in one near the base and in another near the brim. Fill them with water. Compare the distance at which the water streams fall on the ground.
7. Select the simplest experiment to test whether there is any relationship between the power of the magnet and its size.
   a. Take magnets of same shape and different sizes. Find the number of pins which can be attracted by each magnet.
   b. Take four magnets of different shapes. Find the number of pins which can be attracted by each magnet.
   c. Take four magnets of different sizes and shapes. Find the number of pins which can be attracted by each of them.
   d. Take two magnets of same size and different shapes. Find the weight of the iron power that can be attracted by each.
8. Which is the most suitable experiment to test the inference that the depth of the liquid may influence pressure?
   a. Fill water in two jars of different heights. Make bubbles at its bottom by blowing through a straw. Compare the sizes of the bubbles.
   b. Take two jars of same size. Pour water in one of them up to the brim and fill half of the other. Blow slowly such that bubbles arise. Compare the size of the bubbles.

c. fill a jar with water. Make bubbles at its bottom by blowing through a straw. Compare the sizes of the bubbles at different heights from the bottom to the top.
d. compare the size of the bubbles at the bottom of a lake with their size when they reach the surface.

9. Dark and rough plains absorb heat more speedy than white and smooth plains. Suggest a suitable experiment to prove this.
   a. Take two tins of the same size. Paint one black. The other should be polished and painted white. Fill them with water. Note the temperatures and expose them to sunlight. Measure the temperature after fifteen minutes.
   b. Take two tins of the same size. Paint one black. The other should be polished and painted white. Fill them with hot water and note their temperatures. Measure the temperatures after fifteen minutes.
   c. Take two test tubes. Cover one of them with b lack paper. Fill both of them with water and expose to sunlight. After some time measure their temperatures.
   d. Take two test tubes. Cover one of them with paper. Take hot water in both of them. After some time measure the temperature of water in both of them.
10. Which is the most suitable experiment to test the inference that, 'rates of thermal expansion for different substances are different?
   a. Take two compound bars made of iron and copper. Heat one of them up to 200 °C. Compare their lengths.
   b. Take a copper wire and a steel wire of 50 cms length each. Heat them till the temperatures reach up to 200 °C. Measure their lengths.
   c. Take an iron wire and copper wire of different lengths; heat them up to 200 °C. and measure their length again.
   d. Heat two wires of same length and different radius up to 200 °C. Then measure their length.

Test VI

1. A medium is necessary for the propagation of sound. When meteorites collide in the outer space no sound will be heard

even in the surroundings. Te inference that can be drawn from this is……

a. Sound is feeble.
b. The frequency of sound is less than the hearing limit.
c. There is no medium in the outer space to propagate sound.
d. The dust particles in the outer space do not vibrate due to sound.

2. Prakash rolled a small glassy sphere through the floor. When he hit behind it with another glassy sphere its speed increased. When he hit with another from the opposite direction its speed decreased. We can infer from this that………

a. If a force is applied on a body, along the direction of motion, speed increases and if the force is applied in the opposite direction its speed decreases.
b. If a force is applied along the direction of motion, its speed decreases and if the force is applied in the opposite direction its speed increases.
c. The direction of force does not affect the motion.
d. The friction applied against motion decreases its speed.

3. Some scientific experiences of interest are given below.

a. Before throwing the ball, the bowler makes a run up.
b. Before a long jump. An athlete makes a run up.
c. Even when a boy riding on a bicycle stops pedalling the bicycle moves forward some distance.

From these it can be understood that ……..

- Moving bodies have inertia of rest.
- Moving bodies have inertia of motion.
- Moving bodies have a tendency to reach a state of rest.
- Inertia of rest helps to overcome friction.

4. What do you understand from the situations given below?

- A circus performer rides motor cycle inside an iron globe.
- When a bucket containing water is kept revolving at a high speed in a vertical circle, the water does not fall down.

a. The weight of the body is used to provide the centripetal force needed for keeping it revolving.
b. The weight of the body is used to supply the centrifugal force necessary for keeping it revolving.

c. The gravitational force is not being exerted on the body.

d. The moving body is not experiencing weight.

5. Take three tumblers and fill three fourth of each with water. Mark the level of water in them. Put a tea spoon of sodium chloride in the first, sugar in the second and washing soda in the third and stir well. No difference in the level of the water can be seen. What can be seen from these?

a. When a substance dissolves in water, the volume of the solution increases.

b. When a substance dissolves in water, the volume of the solution decreases.

c. There are vacant spaces in between water molecules.

d. When a substance dissolves in water, its temperature decreases.

6. The data collected by a group studying about thunder and lightning are given below.

The altitude of the place (in feet)	Lightning occurs per year
200	10
800	35
1400	55
2000	70
2600	80

What will be the number of lightning per year which occurs at an altitude of 3200 feet?

a. 88

b. 80

c. 75

d. 55

7. Read carefully the scientific experiences given below;

- When we perspire, our dresses get glued to our body.
- A person counting currency notes often wets his fingers to make sure that no two notes remain stick together and thereby left uncounted.
- We find water drops attached to the sides of a tumbler, when it is taken out after dipping in water.

What can you infer from these?

a. There is force of attraction between molecules of different substances.

b. There is force of attraction between molecules of same substance.

c. There is force of repulsion between molecules of different kinds.

d. There is force of repulsion between molecules of same kinds.

8. When a partially inflated balloon was heated to 40°C, its volume was 18 ml. At 50°C, the volume was 230 ml, and at 60°C, the volume was found to be 320 ml. What can you generalize from the given data?

   a. Volume of a gas increases when temperature increases at a constant pressure.

   b. Volume is not affected by the change in temperature.

   c. At constant pressure, there will be no change in the volume.

   d. There is no relation between temperature, volume and pressure of a body.

9. Scrutinise the situation given below.

   - Some insects move easily on the surface of water.
   - A razor blade placed on the surface of water is supported by water film.
   - When a wet paper and a needle are placed on the surface of water, the paper sinks and the needle flats.

The general principle that can be inferred from this is............

   a. Water exerts buoyant force.

   b. The molecules at the water surface attract the object placed on it.

   c. The molecules at the water surface repel the object placed on it.

   d. The free surface of water exerts force to decrease the surface area.

10. The world surrounding us is full of colours. An apple is red, an orange is yellow and leaves are green. What can you conclude from these?

   a. All bodies absorb their own colours and reflect all the other colours.

b. All bodies absorb all colours except their own.
c. Each body can adapt suitable colours.
d. The colour of each body depends on the heat it received from the sun.

Percentile Norms for the Test of Process Outcomes in Physics

Percentiles	*Score in the Test of Process Outcomes in Physics*
P_{10}	15
P_{20}	18
P_{30}	20
P_{40}	23
P_{50}	25
P_{60}	28
P_{70}	32
P_{80}	36
P_{90}	41

Scoring Key for Test of Process Outcomes in Physics

Test I		TEST II		TEST III	
Item no.	Answer	Item no.	Answer	Item no.	Answer
1	c	1	a	1	b
2	b	2	b	2	c
3	d	3	d	3	d
4	d	4	d	4	a
5	c	5	d	5	a
6	c	6	c	6	a
7	a	7	c	7	c
8	b	8	d	8	a
9	d	9	c	9	a
10	b	10	a	10	a

Test IV		TEST V		TEST VI	
Item no.	Answer	Item no.	Answer	Item no.	Answer
1	a	1	b	1	c
2	a	2	b	2	a

3	c		3	a			3	b
4	a		4	b			4	a
5	d		5	a			5	c
6	d		6	a			6	a
7	a		7	a			7	a
8	a		8	d			8	a
9	d		9	a			9	d
10	a		10	d			10	b

References

AAAS (1965). An evaluation model and its application. In science: A Process Approach.

AAAS (1994). Miscellaneous Publications No. 63.6, National Committee on Science.

AAAS (American Association for the Advancement of Science (1968).

AAAS Commission on Science Education (1971). The MAS Project: Science: A Process Approach.

AAAS miscellaneous publication 65-69.

AAAS Miscellaneous Publications no. 63.6. National Committee on Science

AAAS project 2061—Middle grade science text books: A Benchmark-based. http://www.project 2061.org/publication/text book/mgsci/report/research.htm

Adey, P.S. and Harlen, W. (1986). A Piagetian analysis of process skill test items. *Journal of Research in Science Teaching*. 23, 8, 707-726.

Aiello-Nicosia, M.L. *et al.* (1984). The relationship between science process abilities of teachers and science achievements of students; an experimental study. *Journal of Research in Science Teaching*. 21, 8, 853-857.

Ampili, V.P. (1991). A Study of the Relationship of Process Outcomes in Science to Science Interest, Scientific Attitude and Attitude Towards Academic Work of University Entrants. Unpublished M. Phil. Thesis, University of Kerala, Trivandrum.

Anderson J. Elaine (1975). Behavioural objectives, science processes, and learning from inquiry oriented instructional materials. *Science Education*, Vol. 59, 2, 263-271.

Anderson, L.W. and Krathwohl, D.R. (Eds.) (2001). *A Taxonomy for Learning, Teaching and Assessing: A Revision of Bloom's Taxonomy of Educational Objectives*. New York: Adison-Wesley/Longman.

Anderson, R.D. (1970). *Developing Children's Thinking Through Science.* Englewood Cliffs, N.J. Prentice Hall.

Andrew, K.A. (1980). *Construction of a Group Test to Evaluate Secondary School Pupils' Skills in Scientific Processes.* Unpublished Masters Thesis, University of Kerala, Trivandrum.

Antu, Minimol (2000). *Process Outcomes in Basic Science of Primary School Children, An Investigation of Certain Personality Correlates.* Unpublished Doctoral dissertation, school of pedagogical science, M.G. University, Kottayam.

Aruna, N.S. (1981). A study of the Factors influencing the achievement of standard VII students belonging to scheduled castes and scheduled tribes, whose medium of instructions is Kannada, Unpublished doctoral dissertation. Mysore University.

Atkin, J.M. and Karplus, R. (1962). Discovery or invention. *The Science Teacher* 29(2), 121-143.

Baired, W.E. and Borich, G.D. (1987). Validity considerations for research on integrated science process skills and formal reasoning ability. *Science Education*, 71 (2), 259-262.

Bentley, Micheal *et al.* (2007). *Teaching Constructivist Science K-8*, California Corwin Press, Sage Publications Company.

Best, J.W. and Kahn, J.V. (1980). *Research in Education.* (5th edition). New Delhi: Prentice-Hall of India Pvt. Ltd.

Best, John, W. and Khan, James V. (2005). *Research in Education*, New Delhi, Prentice-Hall of India.

Bloom, B.S. (1968). *Taxonomy of Educational Objectives: Handbook.* Cognitive domain, New York: David Mc key company, Inc.

Bloom, B.S., Hastings, J.T. and Madaus, G.F. (Eds.) (1971). *Handbook on Formative and Summative Evaluation of Student Learning.* New York: Mc Graw Hill.

Bruner, J.S. (1962). *The Process of Education.* Cambridge Mass: Harward University Press.

Burns, wise and Okey (1985). A summary Research in Science Education, *Science Education* 69, 3, June 1985.

Carin and Bass (2000). Activities of teaching science as inquiry. http:// www.pearson highered.com/educator/product/methods for teaching science as inquiry.

Carin, A.A. and Sund, Robert, B. (1970). *Teaching Modern Science.* Columbus, Ohio: Charles E. Merrill Publishing Company. A Bell & Howell Company.

Champagne, B. Audrey and Klopfer E. Leopold (1981). Structuring process skills and the solution of Verbal problems involving science concepts. *Science Education.* Vol. 65, 5, 493-513.

Circa (1550BC). The Ebers Papyrus. www.history of information.com

Circa (1600BC). The Edwin Smith Papyrus. www.history of information.com

Cody T. john and Pizzini L. Edward (1976). The effects of a secondary science Training Programme on the methods, procedures and processes of science. *Science Education*. Vol. 60, 2,193-197. Apri-June1976.

Collins, A. (1991). Cognitive Apprenticeship and Instructional Technology. In L. Idol and B.F. Jones (Eds.), *Educational Values and Cognitive Instruction: Implication for Reform* (pp. 121-138). Hillsdale, NJ: Lawrence Erlbaum Associates.

Collins, A. *et al.* (1991) Cognitive Apprenticeship: Making Thinking Visible American Educator, Winter, 1991, *American Educator*, 15(3), 6-11, 38-46. http://www.21learn.org/arch/articles/brown_seely.html

Collins, A., Brown, J.S., and Newman, S.E., (1989). Cognitive Apprenticeship: Teaching the Craft of Reading, Writing Mathematics. In L.B. Resnick (Ed.), *Knowing, Learning and Instruction: Essays in Honour of Robert Glaser*. Hillsdale, N.J. Lawrence Erlbaum Associates, pp. 453-494.

Comber, L.C. and Keeves, J.P. (1973). *Science Education in Nineteen Countriesan Empirical Study*. New York: John Wiley and Sons. Company, Collier Macmillan Ltd.

Conant, J. (1951). *Science and Common Sense: New Haven*. Yale University Press.

Conant, J. (1952). *Modern Science and Modern Man*. New York: Columbia University Press.

Cooper, D. (1986). The GCSE and Chemistry, Chemistry in Britain, May.

Cooper, Joanne. (1991) Telling our own stories: The reading and writing of journals or diaries. In *Stories Lives Tell*, (eds. Witherell, C. and Noddings, N.) New York: Teachers College Press.

COPES (1971). The Conceptually Oriented Programme in Elementary Science.

Cunningham, D. (1984). *Semiosis and learning*. Semiotics 1984, 427-433.

Darrel, B. (1956). The new Basic Science. New York: The Macmillan Company.

DES (1985 a). Science 5-16: A statement of policy. London: H. & MSO.

DES (1985 b). General Certificate of Secondary Education: The National criteria science, London: HMDO.

Devanathan, S. (2010). The Efficacy of Project Based Learning Strategies on Process Outcomes in Biological Science in Correlation with Science Interest. *GCTE Journal of Research of Extension in Education*, 5(2), 58- 63.

Donelly (1983). *Process Approach in Science Teaching*. Bhatt, P.G. (1988), *Science Process skills in Teaching and Learning*. New Delhi: Commonwealth Publishers.

Ebel, R.L. (1969). *Encyclopaedia of Educational Research.* New York: McMillan Book Company.

Ebel, R.L. (1965). *Measuring Educational Achievement.* Englewood Cliffs,

Edison, S.P. (1992). *The Use of Microcomputer Graphics and Alphanumeric Education* 52(2): 197-207.

Eisenkraft (2003). 5E model Expanding. Retrieved on 6th November 2008, http://science.education.nih.gov/houseofreps.

Elementary Science, Rev. 09/2004 I: Curriculum 2005/Science/Elem Science curriculum.doc8

Enger, S. and Yager, R. (1998). *The Iowa Assessment Handbook.* Iowa city: University of Iowa science education centre.

Enger, S. and Yager, R. (2001). *Attitudes Towards Science Inventory.* Thousands Oaks. CA: Corwin Press.

ERIC (1982). Consuegra, Gerard F (1982). Developing Gifted Programmes in Science. (ED236837). http://www.eric.ed.gov/ERICWebPortal/search/basic.jsp

ESS: The Elementary Science Study, (1971).Education Development Centre: Evidence from a Study of Episodic Memory Retrieval: Retrieved on 06th December 2008, http://www.ingentaconnect.com/content/ap/ni.

Finely N. Fred (1982). *An Empirical Determination of Concepts Contributing to Successful Performance of a Science Process: A Study of Mineral Classification.* Vol. 19, 8, 689-696. 1982.

Fitzpatrick, F. (1960). *Policies for Science Education.* New York: Bureau of Publications, Teachers College, Columbia University.

Fitzpatrick, F.L. (1959). The Science Man power project, *Science Education,* Vol. 43, Issue 2, pp. 121-125.

Fraser, J. Barry (1981). Enquiry skill proficiency and socio economic status. *School Science and Mathematics.* Vol. 81, 1, 665-673.1981.

Friedler, Y. Nachmias, R. and Linn, M.C. (1990)/Learning scientific reasoning skills in micro-computer based laboratories. *Journal of Research in Science Teaching,* 27(2), 173-191.

Gagne, R.M. (1967). Science a Process Approach : Purpose, Accomplishments, expectations. Commission on Science education, association for the advancement of science, Washington.

Gagne, R.M. (1970). *The Conditions of Learning.* 2nd ed. New York: Holt, Rinehart and Winston.

Gagne, R.M. (1985). *Conditions of Learning.* New York: Holt, Rinehart and Winston.

Gagne, Robert. (1970) *The Conditions of Learning.* New York: Holt, Rinehart, and Winston.

Geevarughese, G. (2007). School Related Variables and Process Outcomes in Mathematics at the Secondary School Stage. *International Educator,* 19(1), 12-17.

Germann, P.J. (1994). Identifying Patterns and Relationships among the Responses of Seventh Grade Students to the Science Process Skills of Designing Experiments. *Journal of Research in Science Teaching*, 33(1), 79-99.

Germann, P.J. (1989). 'Directed inquiry approach to learning science process skills treatment effects and aptitude treatment interactions. *Journal of Research in Science Teaching* 26, 3, 237-250.

Germann, P.J. and Aram, R.J. (1996). Student Performance on the science Processing of recording data, Analysis of data, Drawing conclusions and providing evidence. *Journal of Research in Science Teaching*. 33, 7, 773-798

Germann, P.J. *et al.* (1996). Identifying patterns and relationships among the responses of seventh grade students to the Science Process skills of designing experiments. *Journal of Research in Science Teaching*. 33, 1, 79-99.

Germann, Paul J. (1994). Testing a Model of Science Process skill Acquisition: an Interaction With Parents Education, Preferred Language Gender, Science Attitude, Cognitive Development, Academic Ability And Biology. *Journal of Research in Science Teaching*. 31, 9, 1003-1021.

Gibels and David (2008) Constructivist learning environments and the impossibility to change student's perceptions of Assessment Demands and Approaches to learning. retrieved on 28th October 2008 http://www.eric.ed.gov/ERIC web portal/Home. Portal

Good, C.V. (1965). *Dictionary of Education*. New York: McGraw Hill Book Company.

Good, C.V. (1969). *Dictionary of Education*. New York: McGraw Hill Book Company.

Good, C.V. (Ed.). (1973). *Dictionary of Education*. New York: Mc Graw Hill Book.

Greeno, J.G. (1988). Situated activities of learning and knowing in Mathematics. Paper presented at the 1988 annual meeting of the PME-NA, Dekalb, IL guides 1 and 2. London: Longman.

Gulati, H.R. (1985). *Fundamentals of General Properties of Matter*, R. Chand & Co., New Delhi.

Hamil, J.B.W. (1994). An Analytical Assessment of Process Skill Proficiencies and Problem Solving Perception of Pre-Service Elementary Science Teacher. *Dissertation Abstracts International*, 55 (ii) 34-65.

Harlen, Wynne, (1989). Recent developments in primary and lower secondary school science. Layton, David (Ed.) *Innovations in Science and Technology Education*, New Delhi: Sterling Publishers Pvt. Ltd.

Henry, W. *et al.* (2007). Analysis of Verbal Interactions an extended open-inquiry general chemistry laboratory Retrieved on 25th October 2008 http://www.eric.ed.gov/ERIC web portal/Home. Portal

Herron, M.D. (1971). The nature of scientific inquiry. *School Review*, 79, 171-212.

http://www.education.shu.edu/pt 3grat/jinicolal skills

Huang, W. (1991). Concept Mapping and Chemistry Achievement, Integrated Science Process skills, Logical Thinking Abilities and Gender at Teachers College in Taiwan. *Dissertations Abstracts International*, 52(3).

Huppert, J. Lomask, S. Michael and Lazarowitz, R. (2002). Computer simulations in the High School: students' cognitive stages, science process skills and academic achievement in microbiology. International Journal of in microbiology. *International Journal of Science Education*, 24(8), August 2002, pp. 803-821.

Hurd, P. and Gallagher, J.J., (1969). *New Directions in Elementary Science Teaching*, Betmount: Wadsworth Publishing Company Inc.

Hurd, Paul Dehart, (1969). *New Directions in Teaching Secondary School Science*: Chicago: Rand Mc Nally and Co.

Hykle, Jacqueline Ann (1994). Interrelationship among cognitive controls, gender, Science content achievement, Science Process skills. *Dissertation Abstract International*, 55, 9, March 1995.

ILEA, (1987). Science in process, Ten units and teachers guide, London: Heinemann.

Jones (1985). A summary Research in Science Education, *Science Education* 69, 3, June 1985.

Jones, Paul Howard, Joiner Richard and Bornford, Jennifer (2006). Theory-prediction consistency and young children's Identification of Causality. International Science 34(2), March 2006, 159-188.

Joseph, Celene (1998). A study of Process Outcomes in Physics in Relation to some Select cognitive, Affective, social and environmental Variables. Doctoral dissertation; Kottayam Mahatma Gandhi University.

Joseph, Celene (2006). ICT in schools: Myths and Realities. Paper presented in the International Conference on Quality Teacher Education through Information Communication Technology 26-29 June, 2006 at St. Christopher's College of Education, Chennai.

Joyce, B. and Weil, M. (1996). *Models of Teaching*. New Delhi: Prentice-Hall of India Pvt. Ltd.

Kaile, N.S. (1988). Intelligence and creativity as predictors of school as the achievement in mother tongue and foreign language at different levels of socioeconomic status. In Buch, M.B. (Ed.), *Fifth Survey of Research in Education*. New Delhi: N.C.E.R.T., 1997.

Karl Pearson. (1937). *The Grammar of Science*. J.M. Dent and Sons Ltd.

Karplus, R. and Thier, H.N. (1971). SCIS: The Science Curriculum Improvement Study.

Karplus, R. and Their, H. (1967). *A New Look at Elementary School Science*. Chicago: Rand Mc Nally.

Khalwania, N.S. (1986). Effectiveness of Concept based Science Curriculum in Developing Cognitive Structures and Acquisition of Process Skills among High School Students. In Buch, M.B. (Ed.), *Fourth Survey of Research in Education*. New Delhi: N.C.E.R.T., 1997.

Klausmeier, H.J. (1980). Learning and teaching concepts—a strategy for testing applications of theory. New York: Academic Press

Klopfer, L.E. (19 7 1). Evaluation of learning in science. Bloom, B.S. *et al.* (Eds). *A Handbook on Formative and Summative Evaluation*. New York: Mc Graw Hill. http://burawoy.berkeley.edu/Methodology/Two%20Methods.T&S.pdf

Klopfer, E.L. (1971). *Individualized science: Relevance for the 1970's* Copyright © 1971 Wiley Periodicals, Inc., A Wiley Company

Kok-Auntoh and Brain, E.W. (1994). Science Process Skills: Are they Generalisable Research in Science and Technological Education, 12.

Kyle, J.R. and William, C. (1980). The distinction between inquiry and scientific inquiry and why high School students should be cognizant of the distinction. *Journal of Research in Science Teaching*, 17(2), 133-139.

Kyle, Jr. *et al.* (1985). What research says: science through discovery: students love It. *Science and Children*. 23, 2, 39-41.

Larkin, J.H. (1983). The role of problem representation in Physics. In D. Gentner and A.S. Stevens (Eds.), *Mental Models*. Hillsdale, NJ: Lawrence Erlabum associates.

Lawrenz, F. and Cohen, H. (1985). The Effect of Methods Classes and Practice Teaching on Student Attitudes Towards Science and Knowledge of Science Processes. *Science Education*. 69(1): 105-113.

Lawson, A., Abraham, M. and Renner. (1989). A theory of instruction: Using the learning cycle to teach science concepts and thinking skills. Manhattan, K.S. National Association for research in science teaching.

Lee and Gosbi (1985). A summary Research in Science Education, *Science Education* 69, 3, June 1985.

Lee, Tien-Ying (1993). Comparison of Cognitive Development, Science Process Skills and Attitude towards Science Among Secondary School Science Pre-service Teachers with Different Science Backgrounds. *Science Education*. 5, September, 1993.

Llewellyn, D. (2007). *Inquire with in Implementing Inquiry-based Science Standards in Grades 3-8*, second edition: California Corwin press, Sage Publications Company.

Lobo, I. (1990). *Effect of Developing Science Process Skills Among Pre-service.*

Macbeth, D.R. (1974). The extent to which pupils manipulate materials and

Mathei's, P.E. *et al.* (1992). A study of the Logical Thinking Skills and

Integrated Process Skills of Junior High School Students in North Carolina and Japan. *Science Education*, 76 (2): 211-222.

Mathur, D.S. (2006). *Elements of Properties of Matter*: Shyamlal Charitable Trust, Ram Nagar, New Delhi.

Mattheis E. Floyd *et al.* (1992). A study of the logical thinking skills and integrated process skills of junior high school students in North Karolina and Japan. *Science Education*, Vol. 76, 2, 210-221, April 1992.

Mayo, P. Donnelly, Nash P.P. and Schwartz, R.W. (1993). Student perception of tutor effectiveness in problem based surgery clerkship. *Teaching and Learning in Medicine* 5(4), 227-233.

McKenzie and Padilla (1985). A summary Research in Science Education, *Science Education* 69, 3, June 1985.

Michaclis, J.U., Grossman, R.H. and Scott, L.F. (1970). *New Designs for Elementary School Curriculum* New York; Mc Graw Hill Inc.

Michalis, J.U. *et al.* (1967). *New Designs for the Elementary School Curriculum*. New York: Mc-Graw-Hall Book Company.

Mills, L.C. and Dean, P.M. (1960). *Problem Solving Methods in Science Teaching*. New York: Buro of Publications.

MINNEMAST (1971). MINNEMAST: *The Minnesota Mathematics and Science Teaching Project*. Mittal Publications.

Modes of Data Presentation with Students' Process Skills and Conceptual Understanding of Genetics. Dissertation Abstracts/international/, 53: 1 1.

Murphy, P. and Gott, R. (1984). The Assessment of frame work for science at NCERT, 1991.

National Committee on Science Education standards and Assessment draft 1994.

National Policy on Education (1986). New Delhi: Ministry of Human Resource Development, New Delhi.

National Policy on Education (1992. National Policy on Education, 1986 (As modified in 1992). www.education.nic.in/natpol.asp. Got. of India, Department of education, Ministry of Human Resource Development, New Delhi. 1998.

Nay, M.A. *et al.* (1971). A Process approach to teaching science. *Science Education*, 53, 2.

NCC (National Curriculum Council) (1991). Science Explorations. York: National Curriculum Council.

NCERT (1982). Integrated science curriculum an introduction. New Delhi.

NCERT (1987). Integrated science curriculum an introduction. New Delhi.

Nedelsky, L. (1965). Science Teaching and Testing. New York: Harcourt, Brace and World, Inc.

Neethu, John (2007). A study on the selected Science Process skills and Creativity of the Students of standard nine of Ernakulam District. M.Ed. Dissertation, Mahatma Gandhi University, Kottayam.

Nemoto, J.S. and Suzuki, K.C. Goal Based Scenario Checklist for Training Application. Retrieved, 26th June 2010, from http://www.engines 4ed.org./hyper book/index.htm New Delhi: NCERT, 1997.

Nuffield 11-13 (1986). How scientists work, how science is used, Teachers' guide.

Nuffield 11-13 (1986) Teachers' guide 1:17 of Education and Science.

Padilla, M.J. (1983). The relationship between science process skills and formal thinking abilities. Journal of Research in science Teaching. 20, 3, 239-246.

Padilla, M.J. (1980). Science activities for thinking. *School Science and Mathematics*, 80, 601-608.

Pappelis, C.K. *et al.* (1980). Can instruction improve science process skills of premedical and pre-dental students. Journal of Research in science teaching. 1, 1, 25-29.

Paulose, P.J. (1987). The influence of certain personality variables, sex and residence on process outcomes in physics of university entrants. Unpublished doctoral Dissertation, University of Kerala Trivandrum.

Paulose, P.J. (1993). Process Outcomes in Learning of Physics of University Entrants: The Role of Manifest Anxiety in Combination with Sex and Residence of subjects. Experiments in Education, 21:66-73.

Piaget, Jean, (1963). *Psychology of Intelligence*. Paterson, N.J. Little fields Adams & Co.

Piburn, M. and Baker, R.D. (1991). Process Skills Acquisition, Cognitive Growth and Attitude Change of Ninth Grade Students in a Scientific Literacy Course. *Journal of Research in Science Teaching*, 28(5), 24-32.

Plomp, T.J. and Ely, P.D. (1996). *International Encyclopaedia of Educational Technology*. (2nd Edition). Cambridge: British Library cataloguing in publication data.

Rachelson, S. (1977) A question of balance: a holistic view on scientific inquiry. *Science Education* 61, 1, 109-115.

Rajan, K.M. (1996). *Science of Science Education*. Kottayam: Learners' offset printers.

Rakow J. Steven (1985). Prediction of the science inquiry skills of Seventeen year olds: a Test of the model of Educational productivity. *Journal of Research in Science Teaching*. Vol. 22, 4, 289-302. 1985.

Ramesh, (1984). Development of objective based science curriculum and to study its efficacy in the acquisition of process skills among high school students. In Buch, M.B. (Ed.). *Fourth Survey of Research in Education*.

Raven, J. Ronald and Sister Calvey Helen (1977). Achievement on a test of Piagte's Operative comprehension as a function of a process oriented Elementary school science programme. *Science Education*. Vol. 61, 2, 159-166.

Richard, D. (2010). An example implementation of Schank's Goal Based Scenarios. Retrieved, 20th June 2010, from http://www.eric.ed.gov/ERIC web portal/Home.portal

Riley P. Joseph (1979). The Influence of hands–on science process training on pre-service teacher's acquisition of process skill and attitude toward science and science teaching. *Journal of Research in Science Teaching*, Vol. 16, 5, 373-384, 1979.

Rogolf, B. (1990). *Apprenticeship in Thinking: Cognitive Development in Social Context*. New York: Oxford University Press.

Rogolf, G. (1984). Thinking and learning in Social context. In B. Rogolf and J. Lave (Eds.), *Everyday Cognition: Its Development in Social Context*. Cambridge MA, Harvard university Press.

Roth, W.M. (1989). Confirmatory factor analysis for validity consideration: a critique. *Science Education*, 73(6), 649-655.

Roth, W.M. and Roy, C.A. (1993). The Development of Science Process skills in Authentic contexts. *Journal of Research in Science Teaching*, 30(2): 127-152.

Royal Society, (1986). A proposal of reduced content for a co-ordinated Science curriculum to age 16. London: The Royal Society.

Saat, Rohaida Mohd (2004). The acquisition of Integrated Science process skills in a web-based learning environment. *Research in Science and Technological Education*. 22(1), May 2004, pp. 23-40.

Saxena, A.K. (1988). *Emerging Perspectives in Physics Education*. New Delhi: Mittel Publications.

Schank, R.C. and Cleary, C. (1995). Engines for education. Retrieved, 20th November 2010. http://www.education.com/goalbased scenario. html

Schank, R.C. and Fano, A. (1995). The Design of Goal Based Scenario. Retrieved, 29th June 2010, from http://www.education.com/goalbased scenario. html

Schmidt, H. (2004) "The Current State of Problem-based Learning," Keynote paper presented at the Problem-based Learning 2004, A Quality Experience. University of Salford, 15-17th September.

Schon, D.A. (1983). *The Reflective Practitioner: How Professionals Think in Action*. New York: Basic Books.

Schon, D.A. (1987). *Educating the Reflective Practitioner*. San Francisco, CA: Jossey Bass.

Science: A Process Approach. New York: Xerox Corporation.

Science Curriculum Elementary (2004) proposed by Catholic schools Office, Diocese of Phoenix attempts to realize the following goals.

Science Process Skills Source: The American Association for the Advancement of Science Retrieved on 25 September 2008.

Screen, P. (1986 b). *Warwick process science*, Southampton: Ashford Press.

Secondary School Teachers on their Classroom Behaviour. Unpublished Doctoral Dissertation, University of Mysore, Karnataka.

Selmes, I. (1978). *Improving Study Skills*, London: Hodder and Stoughton.

Sharma, S. (1982). A Study of Intellectual Factors and Academic Achievement in Arts, Science and Commerce Course at Higher Secondary Stage. In Buch, M.B. (Ed.). *Third Survey of Research in Education*, New Delhi: N.C.E.R.T., 1988.

Shepardson, D.P. (1990). The relationships between problem solving phase, student interactions, and thinking skills among middle school students taught with in the SSCS problem-solving structural model. *Dissertation Abstracts International*, 5 l (9): 3033.

Simon, H.A. (1981). *The Science of the Artificial*, 2nd ed. Cambridge, MA: MIT Press.

Simpson, (1987) Suspect Psychology. *Times Educational Supplement* 3, April.

Simpson, R.D. and Wasik, J.L. (1978). Correlation of Selected Affective behaviours with Cognitive Performance in a Biology Course for Elementary Teachers. *Journal of Research in Science Teaching*, 15(1): 65-71.

Singh, J and Black, P.J. (1991). The effects of task context on pupil's performance n Science Process Skills. *International Journal of Science Teaching*.

Smith, E.W. (Ed.). (1961). *The Educators Encyclopedia*. Englewood Cliffs, N.J. Printince Hall.

Smith. D.J.H. (1986). Do Tests and Examinations Alienate the Gifted Students? *Journal of Gifted Education-Internal* 4: 101-105.

Srawitz M. Barbara and Malone R. Mark (1987). Pre-service Teachers Acquisition and Retention of Integrated science Process skills: A comparison of teacher directed and self instructional strategies. *Journal of Research in Science Teaching*. Vol. 24, 1, 53-59. 1987.

SSCR (1987). *Better Science: Making it Happen*, London: Heinemann/ASE.

SSCR (1987). *Better Science: Twelve Curriculum Guides*, London: Heinemann.

Suresh, K.P. (1991). Identification of certain sociological cognitive and Environmental variables related to Process outcomes in secondary school biology. Unpublished doctoral dissertation; University of Calicut.

Tamir Pinchas and Amir Ruth (1988). Inter relationship among Laboratory process skills in biology. *Journal of Research in Science Teaching*, Vol. 24, 2, 137-144, Feb. 1987.

The Columbia Encyclopedia (1963).

The Conceptually Oriented Programme Project (1969). New York:

The Scottish Education Department Consultative Committee (1969). Science for general education.

Thier, Herbert D. (1973). *Teaching Elementary School Science a Laboratory Approach*. New Delhi: Sterling Publishers Pvt. Ltd.

Tobin Kenneth (1986). Student task involvement and achievement in process-oriented science activities. *Science Education*, 70, 1 61-72 (1986).

Tobin, K.G. and Capie, W. (1982). Relationships between classroom process variables and middle school science behaviour. *Journal of Educational Psychology*, 74, 441-454.

Tomera N. Audrey (1974). Transfer and Retention of transfer of the science process of observation and comparison in junior high school students. *Science Education*, 58, 2, 195-205, 1974.

Tomera N. Audrey (1974). Retention of the science processes of observation and comparison in junior high school students. *Science Education*, 58, 2, 185-193, 1974.

Trends and Problems in Science and Technology Education in Asia. A report of a regional meeting. Singapore July 1976.

Twiss, O.R. (1917). Science Teaching. New York: The Macmillan UNESCO, (1969-70). *New Trends of Integrated Science Teaching*. Vol. 1

Umadevi, M.R. (2008). Effectiveness of Biological Science Inquiry Model on Process Skills in Biology of Secondary School Students. *Experiments in Education*, 36 (10), 13-18.

UNESCO (1993). *New Trends in Chemistry Teaching*. New Delhi: Sterling Publishers Pvt. Ltd.

UNESCO document (1971).

UNESCO *Hand book for Science Teachers* (1980).

UNESCO *Source book for Science in the Primary School* (1992).

UNESCO *Source book for Science Teaching* (1992)

Vaidya, N. (1971). *The Impact Science Teaching*. New Delhi: Oxford and IBH. Publishing Co.

Varghese, P.J. (1989). 'Affective Correlates of Process Outcomes in Biology'. Unpublished M.Ed. Dissertation. University of Calicut

Victor E. and Lemer, M.S. (Eds.). Process Approach. Readings in Science Process outcomes in Physics. Retrieved on is November 2008. http://www.rose-

Wallas (1926). In Ebel (1969). *Encyclopaedia of Educational Research*. New York: McMillan Book Company.

Wallas, Graham (1926). *Art of thought*. New York: Harcourt Barce.

Walter, (1964). *Teaching Science in Today's Secondary Schools*. New Delhi: Prentice Hall of India Pvt. Ltd.

Walters Y. Beaumont and Soyibo, Kola (2001). An analysis of High school students Performance on Five Integrated Science and Technological education 19(2); November 1, 2001, pp. 133-145.

Willington, Jerry (Ed.) (1990). *Skills and Processes is Science Education*.

London and New York: Routledge.

Wilson, G.B. (1996). Cognitive Teaching Models. Retrieved, 20th June 2010, from http://www.engines 4ed. Org/hyperbook/index. Html

Wilson, J.T. (1974). Process of Scientific Inquiry. A Model for Teaching and Learning Science. *Science Education* 58, 1.

Wolman (1973). *Handbook of General Psychology* by Benamine B. Prentice Hall.

Woolnough, B.E. (1995). *Practical Work in Science*. Cambridge University Press.

www-fhs.mcmaster.ca/mhsi/problem-.htm

Yap, K.C. and Yeany, R.H. (1988). Validation of hierarchical relationships among Piagetian cognitive modes and integrated science process skills for different cognitive reasoning levels. *Journal of Research in Science Teaching*, 25(4), 247-281.

Yeany H. Russel, Yap Chin Kueh and Padilla J. Michael (1988). Validation of Hierarchical relationship among Piagetian cognitive Modes and Integrated science process skills for different cognitive reasoning levels. *Journal of Research in Science Teaching*, Vol. 25, 4, 247-281.

Yeany H. Russel, Yap Chin Kueh and Padilla J. Michael (1986). Analyzing Hierarchical relationship among Modes of cognitive reasoning and Integrated science process skills. *Journal of Research in Science Teaching*, Vol. 23, 4, 277-291.

Index

7E learning cycle, 136-141
  elaboration, 139-140
  elicit, 137
  engage, 137–138
  evaluate, 140-141
  explain, 139
  explore, 138
  extend, 140
AAAS, 2, 7, 19, 24, 61, 69, 75, 94
Adey, P.S., 99
Advantages of experiment over observation, 57
Advantages of observation over experiment, 56
Aiello-Nicosia, M.L. , 96
American Association for the Advancement of Science (*see* AAAS)
Amir Ruth, 100
Ampili, V.P. 102
Analogy, 49–51
Analysis and Synthesis, 50
Anderson J. Elaine, 92
Anderson, L.W., 71
Andrew's classification, 80
Application of Scientific Method to the Teaching of Science, 58
Application of the law to new situations, 40
Aristotle, 38, 42
Artificial observation, 54–55
ASEP, 17
Atkin, J.M., 135
Authority and testimony, 57

Baired, W.E., 88–89
Baker, R.D., 101
Basic Processes, 20
Bass, 138–141
Biological Sciences Curriculum Study, 136
Black, P.J., 101
Bloom, B.S., 69
Borich, G.D. , 88–89
Bruner, 6, 8, 28, 62, 122
Burns, Wise, 96

Calvey, 93
Capie, W., 89
Carin and Sund's model, 84
Carin, 138–141
Champagne, 94
Characteristics – Scientific attitude, 13
Chemical Bond approach, 17
Chemical Education Material Study, 17
Circa 1550 BC, 38
Circa 1600 BC, 38
Cody T. John, 92
Cognitive domain, 69, 71
Cohen, H., 96
Collecting data, 25, 68, 80
Collection of data, interpretation of data, and formulation of hypotheses, 40
Collection of facts and data, 54
Columbia Encyclopaedia, 6
Comber, L.C., 169
Communicating, 7, 22, 26, 34, 36, 82
Conant, 6, 8
Concept Attainment Model, 122–127
  exemplars, 122–123
  instructional effects, 131
  nurturant effects, 132
  principles of reaction, 126
  reception model, 123–124
  selection model, 124
  social system, 126

support system, 126–127
syntax, 125–126
unorganized material model, 124–125
variations of the 123–125
Conceptual structures, 66
Conceptually Oriented Programme in Elementary Science, 17, 21
Controlled variables, 36, 56
Cooper, D., 62
Criteria of good hypothesis, 52
Cunningham, D., 88

Dean, P.M., 68
Defining Operationally, 5
Dependent variable, 56, 94–95, 170
Designing investigations, 35–36
Devanathan, S., 106
Dewey, John, 61, 67
Directional hypothesis, 53
Discovery approach, 18
Donnely, 61

Ebel, R.L., 68, 171
Edison, S.P., 102
Eisenkraft, 136
Elementary School Science Project, 17
Elementary Science Study, 17, 27
Elements of concepts, 122, 127
Elements of Scientific Method, 42
ERIC, 65
Establishment of the law, 40

Facts, 8, 54, 109, 115, 119, 149
Finely N. Fred, 95
Fitz Patrick, 6
Formulating hypotheses, 51, 104, 168, 170
Fraser J. Barry, 95
Friedler, Y. Nachmias, 89

Gagne, R.M., 3–4, 7, 9, 20, 72–73, 88
Gagne's Hierarchy of Learning Types, 72–73
attitude, 73
chaining, 72
cognitive strategies, 73
concept learning, 72
discrimination learning, 72
intellectual skills, 72–73
motor skills, 73
problem solving, 72
rule learning, 72
signal learning, 72
stimulus response learning, 72
verbal association, 72
verbal information, 73
GCSE, 62
Geevarughese, G., 105
Generalization of the law, 40
Germann, P.J., 100
Goal Based Scenario Model, 148, 150
Good, C.V., 65
Gosby, 97
Greeno, J.G., 89

Habits of Mind, 24, 26
Hamil, J.B.W., 103
Harlen, W., 99
Harvard Physics Project, 17
Henry Poincore, 6
Herron, M.D., 89
Hierarchical Nature of Science Process Skills, 88
Horrace, 64
Huppert, J. Lomask, 104
Huxley, 6
Hypothesis, 10, 34, 51–52, 169
Hypothetico-deductive reasoning., 88

Idealization and abstraction, 40
Independent variable, 56, 93, 95, 101, 104
Inquiry approach, 2, 4–5, 94, 100
Inquiry training model, 130–132
Integrated Processes, 21
Interpreting data, 80
Investigative approach, 5

Jones, P.H., 22, 97, 105
Joseph, Celene, 103, 105
Joyce, B., 61, 122, 125

Karl Pearson, 40
Karplus, R., 135
Keeves, J.P., 169
Khalwania, N.S., 99
Klopfer, E.L., 3–4, 69, 75
Klopfer's Classification of Outcomes in Science , 75

Kok-Aunton, 103
Krathwohl, 69
Krathwohl, D.R., 71

Landmark Education Improvement Act, 24
Larkin, J.H., 89
Lawrenz, F., 96
Lawson, A., 97, 135
Lee, 97
Lesson Plan Based on 7E Learning Cycle, 141–46
Lesson Plan Based on Goal Based Scenario Model, 149
Lesson Plan by Using Concept Attainment Model, 127–100
Lesson Plan on ITM, 132–134
Lobo, I., 101
Logical process, 40

Macbeth, D.R., 91
Major concepts, 66
Major curricular innovations focussed on Science process, 17–18
Malone R. Mark, 100
Mathematical reasoning, 22
McKenzie, 97
Mills, L.C., 68
Minnesota Mathematics and Science Teaching Project, 17, 22
Minor premise, 42

National Policy on Education (1992), 1
National Science Teachers Association, 24
Natural observation, 54
NCERT, 64
Nedelsky, L., 69, 73, 169
Nedelsky's Competence- Ability Classification in Science Learning
Non-directional hypothesis, 53
Nuffield courses, 17
Nuffield Science Curriculum Project, 35

Padilla, 97
Pappelis, C.K., 94
Paul P. Jyothis, 104
Paulose, P.J., 99, 103
Physical Science Study Committee, 17–18
Piaget, Jean, 4, 31, 86, 88–89, 93
Piaget's Model of Intellectual Development, 86–88
  The concrete operational stage, 88
  The formal operational stage, 88
  The pre-operational stage, 87
  The sensorimotor stage, 87
Piburn, M., 101
Pizzini L. Edward, 92
Predictability, 40
Problem Based Learning, 154–1160
  Lesson Plan Using Problem Based Learning Strategy, 157–160
  Methodology of Problem Based Learning, 156-157
Process Models, 84
Process of Science (Nay, Marshal and others), 77
Process vs Product Approach, 66

Rakow J. Steven, 96
Relationship between process and products of science, 12
Revised Bloom's Taxonomy, 71
Rogolf, B., 89
Roth, W.M., 89, 102

Saat, Rohaida Mohd, 105
Schank, R.C., 147
Schmdit, H., 155
Schon. D.A., 89
School Science Curriculum Project, 17
Science – a body of knowledge, 8
Science – a method of inquiry, 11
Science- a way of investigation, 11
Science – a way of thinking, 13
Science – an attitude towards life, 13
Science a Process Approach (SAPA), 2, 17–21, 91, 94
Science Curriculum Improvement Study, 17, 30, 136
Science in Process, 17, 37
Science processes, 1, 65
Scientia, 6
Scientific and Critical Thinking, 11
Scientific attitude, 2–3, 6, 13–14, 16, 75–76, 102, 142
Scientific literacy, 14

Shepardson's Identification of Science Processes, 83–84
Simon, H.A., 88
Simpson, 63
Singh, J., 101
Srawitz M. Barbara, 100
Strategies and Sample Lesson Plans for Developing Science Process Skills, 107–122
  Constructivist Teaching Strategy, 108
  Lesson Plan Based on Constructivist approach, 108–112
  Cognitive Apprenticeship Model, 113–114
  Lesson Plan Based on Cognitive Apprenticeship Model, 115–122
  Zone of proximal development, 113
Studies on process skills, 91
Suresh, K.P., 101

Tamir Pinchas, 100
Taxonomical Approaches in Defining Educational Objectives, 69
Teaching Strategies in Cognitive Apprenticeship, 114
  Coaching, 114
  Modeling, 114
  Scaffolding, 114
Tennessee Science Curriculum Framework, 24
Test of graphing in science, 97
Testing of Hypothesis, 53
Testing of Science Process Skills, 161–197
  checklists, 163
  direct and indirect assessment, 162
  inquiry reports, 166
  interview, 163
  investigation reports, 167–168
  rating scale on reflection on learning through inquiry reports, 167
  science journals, 165–166
  techniques for performance based assessment, 163-165
  test of process outcomes in physics, 168–172
  preparation of items, 169
  recognising and defining problem, 168
  formulating hypotheses, 168
  collecting data, 168
  interpreting data, 169
  evaluation of hypotheses, 169
  formulating generalisations, 169
  discriminating power
  difficulty index, 172
  item analysis
  validity, 172
  reliability, 172
The National Policy on Education (NPE, 1986), 2
The nature of science, 7, 14–16, 66–67
The Role of Science Teacher in Promoting Scientific Literacy, 14
Their, H., 135
Theorem, 10
Theoretical account, 9
Thier, Herbert D. (1973
Tobin Kenneth, 99
Tobin, K.G., 89
Tomera N. Audrey , 91
Types of hypotheses, 53

Umadevi, M.R., 105
UNESCO Approach Relating to Process Outcomes, 80
UNESCO document (1971), 68
Unifying Concepts, 24, 26
Using numbers, 5, 34
Using Space/time Relationship

Varghese, P.J., 100

Wallas, Graham, 68
Warwick Process Science, 17
Welsch Science processes Inventory, 93
Willington, Jerry, 63
Wilson's model, 86
Wolman, 65

Yap, K.C., 89, 98
Yeany, R.H., 89, 98